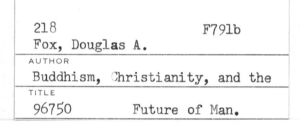

BUDDHISM, CHRISTIANITY, AND THE FUTURE OF MAN

BUDDHISM, CHRISTIANITY, AND THE FUTURE OF MAN

by Douglas A. Fox

THE WESTMINSTER PRESS
Philadelphia

ISBN 0–664–20937–8

LIBRARY OF CONGRESS CATALOG CARD NO. 70–189123

Acknowledgments

The National Council of Churches, Division of Christian Education, for Scripture quotations from the Revised Standard Version of the Bible, copyrighted 1946, 1952.

Oxford University Press, Inc., and Cambridge University Press, for quotations from *The New English Bible.* © The Delegates of the Oxford University Press and The Syndics of the Cambridge University Press 1961, 1970.

PUBLISHED BY THE WESTMINSTER PRESS ®
PHILADELPHIA, PENNSYLVANIA

PRINTED IN THE UNITED STATES OF AMERICA

Library of Congress Cataloging in Publication Data

Fox, Douglas A   1927–
   Buddhism, Christianity, and the future of man.

   Bibliography: p.
   1. Man (Theology) 2. Man (Buddhism) I. Title.
BT702.F68   218   70–189123
ISBN 0–664–20937–8

FOR MY PARENTS

For each age is a dream that is dying,
Or one that is coming to birth.
                    —*Arthur O'Shaughnessy*

Contents

Contents

Introduction

Man is an animal who dreams. He does not live contented with only the furnishings of stark fact, with the present as his only home. Even if he speaks of belonging to the "Now" he rarely means that this "Now" is a static, stable, accomplished, and entirely satisfying place to stand; he means that it is the place in which he moves and tries to realize a dream.

It is his dreaming that makes a man available to religious adventure and experience.

A historic irony is the fact that when Charles Darwin proposed, in the field of biology, a theory of general evolution (a concept richly religious in suggestion) he was opposed by, among others, certain ardently religious people who preferred the notion of man as instantly perfected. Instantaneous completion, even though a crudely literalistic reading of Old Testament myths may seem to endow it with Biblical support, is really a nonreligious and at best very doubtfully Biblical concept. For man's dream is evolutionary. He envisions himself as somehow incomplete, as moving toward a goal, as a process and not a fixed and finished product. It is thus that, by and large, the Bible also sees him, and this is not surprising, for it is man's longing for fulfillment which is the basis for a reaching beyond the factual and momentary "is" which, in turn, is midwife to the birth of religious sensitivity.

Within the traditions of the great formal "religions" [1] there

are two primary modes in which this process to completeness
has been viewed: there is one which sees an essential continuity embracing man and his ultimate object of devotion
(which is simultaneously his goal). Man and his God, his
Absolute, his Vision are continuous, and the attainment of
perfection is really a matter of overcoming delusion, ignorance,
fallacious judgments. And there is a view that sees between
man and the Ultimacy toward which he looks for meaning
and fulfillment a *dis*continuity. For this view, man's process
demands not merely the elimination of ignorance or miscon-
ception but the crossing of a gulf, an actual movement and
transformation. Where the first mode of thought may speak of
the final attainment as a discovery of what always and everywhere is the Truth, as a "becoming aware," and an "awakening" or "enlightenment," the second (although it may, with
qualification, use those terms too) speaks of "new birth" or
"reconciliation."

For most Westerners, I believe, the most viable version of
the first type of religious orientation mentioned above is
Mahayana Buddhism in one of its sects, and of the second,
some type of Christianity. It is the purpose of this book to
examine these ancient but living alternatives in order to see
whether they really offer a coherent framework for the dreaming of modern man or whether, as many believe, they are now
bankrupt and made obsolete by the conditions in which we
live.

It will not be enough, of course, to consider Buddhism and
Christianity simply in their usual formulations, answering com-
fortably the questions of an earlier age. Man's dream is an
uneasy one, disturbed by new understandings, hopes, alarms,
and challenges. We shall begin, then, by an examination of
the conditions in which our dream must now take shape, and
move from that to the traditions we are concerned with, asking them the questions which the shifting images of our dream
engender.

Let us be clear about our purposes in all of this. We want,

first, to see whether two great and representative religious orientations can, separately or together, speak meaningfully to us today. If they cannot, then it is clear that we ought to recognize that a long chapter in man's history is over, and we should willingly (although maybe sadly) turn the page and hope for something new. Secondly, if any value does remain in these traditions, it may be hoped that the present book will encourage a little the growing dialogue between their adherents, for out of such a confrontation may come increasing light and understanding.

In concentrating on Mahayana and Christianity we do not wish to imply that no other tradition has the possibility of meaningfulness, but we acknowledge that any book must have its limits, and we suggest that of all the great religious modes of living, for better or for worse, these are the two most likely to capture the allegiance of Western people today and to give their civilization the depth and coherence for want of which it presently languishes. If they fail, then it is doubtful whether any existing formal religion can succeed, for between these two there are offered in clear terms the major alternative ways in which man, in the context of a traditional religious expression, may grasp and strive to realize his ultimate dream.

One final word of explanation is needed. Although the writer is a Christian of a sort, he does not pretend to be presenting here *the* Christian view of anything. It is probably impossible to do so. Rather, he offers *a Christian's* view of certain matters. Similarly, although he has spent considerable time in sympathetic study of Buddhism, to the point of allowing it to challenge his Christian commitment, he cannot offer *the* Buddhist view. Instead, he has tried to immerse himself in the data and the experience of Buddhism that he might present here what he thinks most worth saying from within that context.

Part One
QUESTIONING

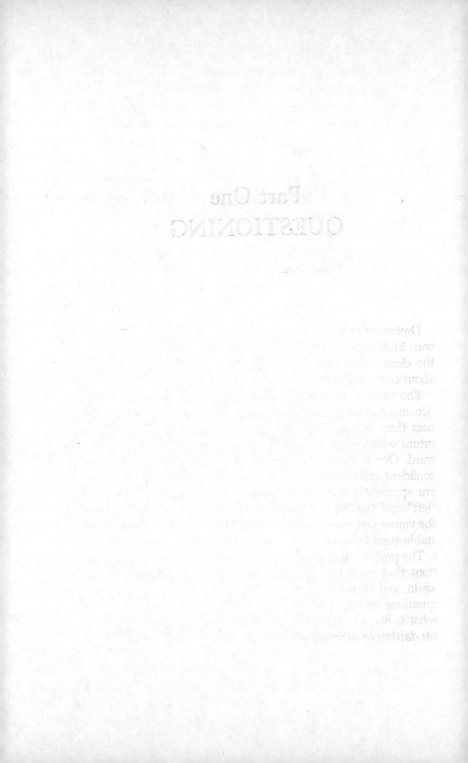

I

Prospects and Questions

What dreams may come . . . ?
—*Shakespeare,*
Hamlet, *Act III, Scene i*

Dreaming is not so simple or so satisfying now as once it was. Shifting currents of doubt and of frenzy move through the dream and blur its images, for we are no longer clear about our possibilities.

The truth is, we are not sure what we are or what we may become, so that although we are no less aware of incompleteness than before, we cannot easily project an image of our future which wins our confidence and moves us strongly forward. Our motions now are alternately sluggish and frantic, confident and alarmed. Our societies in the western hemisphere are apparently increasingly marked by serious divisions—the "left" and the "right," the revolutionary and the reactionary, the young and the old—but there is little evidence of calm and stable confidence in the dreams of any side.

The problem is that we have some new and unresolved questions that must be answered before clear hope can be ours again, and even before we can begin to answer those ultimate questions which open the door to hope: *What is man? And what is his appropriate mode of being in the world? What is his destiny or ultimate possibility?*

What, then, are the unanswered preliminary questions? They arise from some new knowledge, new hypotheses, and consequent new uncertainties which the remarkable achievements of the nineteenth and twentieth centuries have brought to us, and for the sake of convenience we shall arrange them in four general categories: Human *Being*; Technology; Politics and Individual Significance; God and Human Experience.

HUMAN *Being*

Men once believed themselves to be irreducible mysteries, the supreme handiwork of an inscrutable God who alone could have fashioned them so ingeniously and breathed into them the breath of life. With such an origin, it was easy to believe themselves cosmic princes, heirs of the divine, destined for greater glory than anyone had ever seen. But after pride came the fall. The theory of general evolution raised to prominence by Darwin and developed by a generation of successors has modified the concept of man's uniqueness so that, to retain his former hopes, he has now to assume that his enigmatic Creator has chosen a strangely tortuous road as the means of his creation.

Still, it was possible to believe that man was the possessor of a mind and a soul which separated him from other creatures. Life itself, forever (it was assumed) beyond definition or manipulation, was evidence enough of a Hand at work in the universe, and therefore in man, which guaranteed the fulfillment of our immortal longings. To be sure, there were problems that grew steadily sharper as the nineteenth century went its way. The discovery, even by readers of popular journals, of "primitive" societies where men did not come into life recognizably trailing clouds of glory yet were indisputably *men* may have been mildly discomforting for a few. Furthermore, the fact that God had ordained the sexual act as our only means of procreation must, to some of our Victorian forefathers, have betrayed a singular lack of celestial sensitivity.

But God moves in mysterious ways and it is not absolutely necessary that he be a Gentleman. We, for our part, do our best with what he has given us, assured of our immortal grandeur. Moreover, now that we were evolutionists we could believe that "every day in every way" we were getting better and better.

The nineteenth century, which saw men plugging the leaky dike of their high self-estimate with the frantic finger of rational compromise or the arrogant fist of competitive individualism, is dead, and the twentieth has curiously rebuilt the dike while simultaneously undermining it. Two world wars, a major economic depression, the exposure of the "smoke-filled room" as the place and means of political decision, have all contributed to a pervasive discomfiture. New discoveries of human capacities for ingenuity and for viciousness, for objectivity and for self-deception, have elated and dismayed us. But, most troublesome of all, science has begun to probe in places that we thought inviolable and, while it raises us to new peaks of pride in our accomplishment, it also makes us uneasily aware that many of the comforting assumptions about ourselves which we had somehow salvaged from the recent past are eroding in our hands.

In 1952 a chemist named S. L. Miller allowed a mixture of hydrogen, ammonia, methane, and water to circulate in the presence of an electrical discharge for about one week. At the end of this time his mixture was found to contain several organic compounds, including amino acids, which had not been there at the beginning of the experiment. The significance of this is that the proteins of the human body are constructed from amino acids, and it is at least possible that Miller had reconstructed in his laboratory conditions similar to those which existed on the surface of our planet in a very remote past. Thus he may have reproduced experimentally the first step in the production of human life.

Suddenly man's romantic image of himself, or rather of his *life*, as nobly mysterious seems threatened. Are we, after all, merely the product of purely casual chemical circumstances? Was it not more flattering to think that our progenitor had been carefully and lovingly created in the hands of a God who breathed his own breath into him, thus conferring a "life" that owed nothing to mundane chemistry? Are we not all made trivial by Miller's genius? Of course, we can think of God as the original cosmic Chemist, but deity in a starched white coat is less appealing than a tender Father, and somehow the feeling lingers that a skeleton in our ontological cupboard has uncouthly disclosed itself.

It may still be felt that however casual its origin, the present form and content of human life is a matter for great wonder and, since the development of molecular biology, the arena of such incredible possibilities that we can dismiss the memory of our lowly beginnings, much as an Australian dismisses the penal origin of his nation, and build a dream upon the prospect of a future we ourselves may largely shape. It is becoming possible to look forward to a day when the biological aspects of our life shall be determined not by chance, by inescapable heredity, or by *karma*, but by a process of genetic engineering which shall have preserved us from the power of destructive genes and ensured for us the physical basis of a productive, healthy, and intelligent life. Whether this shall be accomplished by selective mutation by means of specific mutagens or (more likely, I gather) through the introduction of new "messenger" RNA molecules to transform a cell in some desirable fashion, or in yet some other way is hardly the issue at present. *Some* method of effective "bioengineering" will undoubtedly be developed, giving us a power undreamed by our predecessors, to shape our communal destiny.

The importance of the emerging possibility of the control of selection or performance of human genes is not hard to see. At present about 4 percent of all babies show evidence of some genetic defect, and this is not surprising when it is estimated that humans carry an average of from four to eight recessive *lethal* genes, or even more that are defective in a milder degree. The occurrence of a matched pair of such disastrous genes is therefore a possibility in the conception of virtually any baby. The hope that molecular biology is offering us is, then, that we may be able to predict and eliminate the occurrence of such genetic misadventures as mental retardation or physical deformity, and even that we may be able to direct our own evolution as a species.

To what we have said, add the already aging fact of organ transplants in the human body, and our potential capacity for designing and, when necessary, rebuilding ourselves seems almost infinite! It will increase further as we develop the use of nonhuman and even inorganic materials for the repair of our bodies, and this is no remote possibility or wild speculation of science fiction: already there are hundreds of persons living and working because of artificial heart valves which are partly made of Teflon! One supposes that such persons must beware of ingesting scouring pads, but this is a small price to pay for continuing effective existence.

It is not only physical well-being that we may one day be able to determine. Even the happiness of man may become a factor he can manipulate at will. In principle it is even now possible to determine an individual's emotional condition by means of electrodes strategically implanted in his brain, and to control these efficiently and neatly either by his own effort or from a remote operations center. Tranquillity, joy, and even, apparently, the Zen state of *satori* can be artificially induced or may come to be possibilities with some further experiment. The "pursuit of happiness" may thus one day no longer be an empty phrase fit only for a great national document but the description of a fulfilled stage of social engineering.

Indeed, the road to universal happiness may not even require surgery. By simple processes of conditioning, it may, so some psychologists believe, be possible to produce a society whose people enjoy what they may have and, being content with what they can achieve, live in peace, experiencing no wants that are not easily satisfied.

What a creature is man! He has learned to release the power of the atom; he searches with amazing instruments the silent shores of distant stars; he forces the unwilling earth to yield its secrets and its riches; and he dreams that one day he will bend other planets to his purposes. And now, this master of his universe can begin to design his own descendants. It is no wonder that many people today are impatient with any talk of limitations, and easily repudiate old-fashioned religious notions of "sin" or other expressions of human weakness and inadequacy. We brace our shoulders, throw back our heads, and shout from the rooftops that the world has "come of age"! Man no longer gropes like a star-struck child in weakness and mystery. We have no need of God, the cosmic Father and Holder of all frantic hands, for we have become as gods ourselves.

Yet one thing more must be said of us. For all but the insensitive, there is sometimes a hint of hollowness about our boasting. Whatever knowledge and power we have, we remain finite. Time holds us "green and dying," and the skull still grimaces beneath the lively freshness of our cheek. Indeed, the chill suggestion haunts dark corners of our mind that our very triumphs may themselves be steps to our undoing, and that our pinnacle of pride may be another Babel.

It is not merely the fact that we are temporary that dismays us. There is also the insignificance of our place in the universe. When men believed that God had created the entire cosmos as a setting for his masterpiece—themselves—they felt comfortable and at home. But now we know too much. We are like ants aboard the ocean liner of our galaxy, floating in a wide black sea, and it is our manifest unimportance that impresses us. As W. H. Auden has observed with regard to current theories about our gigantic and expanding universe:

> Who
> Would feel at home astraddle
> An ever expanding saddle? [2]

Moreover, the universe itself has lost status for some of us because it seems so meaningless. What purpose does it serve? The vaster part of it seems to exist with no reference or relevance to life; incredible quantities of energy and matter churning spectacularly in complete futility! Can we suppose that a dear old Unseen Hand has organized the Greatest Show on Earth (or anywhere else) so that for a fleeting moment in an otherwise wasteland of eternity we privileged mortals may lend our boggling attention to one fragment of the scene? Even if we could believe that this were true, what a waste that so much of the performance was over before we arrived, and so much of it will be staged after our reluctant departure!

If we look dispassionately at the evidence of the universe, are we not entitled to conclude that we are unwanted and accidental products of a mindless and unaccountable process?

However, quantity is not quality, and we may hope that it is in the latter that we excel. We are small and brief, but still our powers are exciting, especially the measure of control we now can exercise over our own destiny. Or are there here, too, uneasy questions to be asked?

It is well enough to gloat about human organ transplants, but how shall we think about ourselves, how value ourselves, if it appears that we are rather like a tree whose branches can be grafted upon another? An exchange of hearts or kidneys, although remarkable, perhaps raises few serious questions of philosophy, but what of the transplanting of a brain? This organ of consciousness, of recognition and self-awareness: can it be passed around from one to another without a serious question of identity and value arising? Are we this recognizable face and figure, or are we that capacity for thought and memory? Above all, are we simply a set of replaceable parts, our only value their efficiency? Or are we valuable only for what we can produce?

It is wonderful, of course, that we can learn to prevent genetic defects and produce, someday, an "optimal" human being. But does this mean that we have now become no more

remarkable than the machines we are also gradually perfecting? Are we, in fact, merely ingenious machines that can design
better ones?

Nor would our most serious questions become irrelevant
even if our science finally defeated man's last enemy, death
itself. Certainly we can expect at least much longer lives for
some future generation. The study of geriatrics may discover a
way to suspend in our bodies the aging process, and automated
traffic controls may virtually eliminate accidents on the roads.
We may succeed in avoiding war, and we may finally conquer
every vicious microbe upon the earth. But what would these
achievements mean? Is a man's life to be measured by its
length or by its quality? If mere survival is all that matters to
us, then maximal man is, after all, not much better than minimal
mouse.

No, the questions that haunt us throughout every rehearsal
of our remarkable achievements are questions about meaning,
quality, value. What sort of man is he who will belong to a
society in which, by conditioning or remote control, we are all
happy? May we dream of our future with hope and joy, or
must we dread the nightmare of Aldous Huxley's *Brave New
World* and Anthony Burgess' *A Clockwork Orange*?

In short, our recent achievements of knowledge and skill
have raised again some very old questions. What does it mean
to be a man? Once our dream was built upon the belief that
God had made us in his image and that there was something
inviolable about our dignity and individuality and value. Imperfect we knew ourselves to be, but the design was magnificent, and God and we together would fulfill it. Today we
see ourselves as potentially making our successors, not necessarily in *our* image, but in one of our choosing and we no
longer believe we can borrow a blueprint from God. Is this, if
it is not illusion, our greatness? If so, is it also the indication
of our triviality, and is all our self-perfecting only the paltry
self-manipulation of doomed gnats whose pain and sorrow and
fear are only cosmic incidents, barely perceptible creakings of

the monstrous machine? Is even our last virtue—endurance—no merit but a pointless passion?

And, in the end, is death the final, inescapable mockery reducing our entire adventure to the strange absurdity of a galactic hiccup?

For all our power, we know ourselves to be painfully incomplete, and most of us find it hard to shape a dream out of the self-knowledge that is newly ours. Perhaps this is why so many people today, young and old, are (as the sociologists say) no longer goal-oriented but role-oriented. There are no goals in which they can honestly believe; there are only present roles to fill and play out to the end.

TECHNOLOGY

Our age is distinguished not only by the new powers that man is gaining over his body and mind but by the expansion of his control over the environment. Even primitive societies adapt the environment to their human needs—for instance, by digging irrigation ditches or building simple shelters—but the development of technology in the twentieth century challenges the most lively imagination. Distance is no longer an impediment to human encounter, because it can so easily be overcome. On land and sea and in the air we move at speeds that our grandparents once thought impossible, and our acceleration is by no means ended. We may look forward to traveling in aircraft capable of breaking not only the ill-fated *sound* barrier but that of *heat* as well, and doing it while all routine decisions and control are effected by computers. Automation of traffic control and maintenance, as well as of flying itself, may lead to an era in which maximum suborbital speed is matched for us by maximum safety.

On the ground we may expect to have motorways equipped with guidance and detector devices that will allow electronic control of our vehicles and make us almost as safe on the highway as in the air! Thus every corner of our globe will at last become accessible to the weekend voyager, and eventually we shall visit other planets to satisfy contemporary Alexanders.

The industrial revolution has entered a new phase altogether with the development of cybernation and automation and their promise to us of an effortless and affluent future in which machines serve us as incredible and uncomplaining slaves, saving our muscles and our brains from useless and tedious labor. Work that would once have been done only with almost infinite time and effort will become a matter of instant accomplishment by the gentle pushing of a button, and we shall no longer have to rely on faith to move our mountains.

Communications between distant persons and governments will be dazzling in their speed and accuracy, although this does not guarantee an improvement in the quality of their content. The possibility of the storage, speedy recovery, and almost immediate dissemination of vast quantities of information may well make privacy a legend. It will, for instance, become possible before long for authorities to be much more effectively aware of what persons are doing and saying. Even now income-tax evasion is becoming more difficult in the United States because the Internal Revenue officers are beginning to employ a large computer system which will eventually keep track of every transaction that should result in the paying of tax. Obviously computer surveillance can be—and therefore doubtless will be—extended to many areas of our lives, and the time may well come when a seizure of the official computer will constitute the seizure of government.

We have mentioned, as illustrations, only a few areas in which technology may be expected to continue its dramatic advance and to change the pattern of our lives. There is a great deal here for which we must feel human pride and satisfaction, yet even these accomplishments raise some problems. The stark truth is that although our inventiveness may provide for us an environment which is, in every material respect, a latter-day Garden of Eden, we are sometimes dimly aware that there are serpents lurking in it: we may live one day in a golden paradise, but something in us says: Beware! There is malice in wonderland!

Marshall McLuhan speaks of technology as an "extension of man" and optimistically looks forward to new levels of "participation" as worldwide communication networks are established, and to new freedom as men are progressively delivered by machines from drudgery. But if a man has within himself not only peaceful and constructive attitudes but also vindictiveness, sadism, masochism, the desire to exploit his neighbor, and simple selfishness, will not his "extensions" extend the possibilities for these too?

Indeed, we are already in trouble. Our increasingly efficient industries are inexorably polluting the air we breathe and the water we drink; we may consume recklessly the products of the seas and rivers of the world; we may exhaust our soil; we may destroy natural species and natural beauty in pursuit of the thrills of killing or acquiring. With a monumental failure of restraint we may cover the earth with people who have nothing left to eat but each other. All these dangers are within our reach, and technology does not automatically relieve or intensify them, but may do either as it is used wisely or foolishly.

Certain it is that automation will save us from much drudgery. But *for* what will it save us? The Protestant Ethic has taught us for several generations that work, especially economically productive work, is virtue, and we are uneasy if we are not earning money, so how shall we avoid neurosis if we are set free from the need and opportunity to spend much of our time doing so? Is some other criteria of self-estimation possible for us, so that we can enjoy guiltlessly the leisure we may be forced to accept?

The development of technology in even the next twenty years promises to change our lives enormously. There is nothing inherently disturbing about this, provided the changes are part of a viable vision that is based on a concept of man which we can endorse. Technology must help us to fulfill our dream if it can, and at least it must not transform it into a nightmare. The question is, What sort of dream may be dreamed by men with the capacity we have been discussing?

We must learn to use our tools wisely so that they will enhance our humanity. But what *is* our humanity? We can never control our machines for our own good until we know what our own good is, and here, again, our understandings of ourselves, and our dreams of what we may become, are vague. We must fashion a dream that takes stock of *all* the moral possibilities of men and is not beguiled by our strengths alone. We need a clearer understanding of our relation with the rest of nature as well as with other persons, because in our dealing with both we face new responsibilities in an age when our skills and our tools enable us to heal or destroy as never before. How droll if the final consequence of our explorations in space is the establishment on some distant star of the common cold!

Technology can enrich us, but if it is used badly, without regard for whatever truly makes us human and for the general good of universal nature, or used by those who would control men for nefarious ends, it can destroy qualities of life without which we shall be poor indeed.

In short, we need a set of values by which we can direct the use of our technical skills, and these values are not implicit in the skills themselves nor in the sciences that lie behind them. Where shall we find direction?

POLITICS AND INDIVIDUAL SIGNIFICANCE

It was a cliché of the 1950's that contemporary men and women, especially the young, faced a crisis of identity. "Who am I?" was the prevailing cry on college campuses, and churches led their young people to conference after conference where they were invited to enjoy an orgy of introspection. With the next decade the dominant question changed. No longer was the pressing concern one of identity but one of significance. The suggestion now is that even if we knew who we were, it would make no difference. We are minute parts of an uncontrollable social machine in a vast and uncontrollable universe, and what we are and what we do make no ripple on the sea of Being.

Technology has helped to make us know our insignificance, for ours is an era of multiple records that flow through the veins of computers, and these, themselves impersonal, conspire to deny personal reality to all of us. Wherever I turn I find myself reduced to a number. My vital and not so vital statistics are comprehended on small cards (holed but unholy), devoured by machines which thereupon classify me, categorize me, determine my admission to college, my suitability for employment and promotion—in short, my place and my destiny. One may laugh, but only uncomfortably, at W. H. Auden's poem "The Unknown Citizen (To JS/07/M/378 This Marble Monument Is Erected by the State)," for in this the poet summarizes the data recorded by the state concerning the life of a carefully observed typical citizen of the future (but not the *distant* future). The data is statistical and generalized, utterly devoid of any suggestion that its subject was a unique human being, and the poem concludes:

Was he free? Was he happy? The question is absurd:
Had anything been wrong, we should certainly have heard.[3]

The mood engendered by this apparent loss of individual significance is one of the things against which young people rebel, although the form of their rebellion is often ambiguous. Two characteristics of the youthful revolt of the late 1960's were its generally amorphous character, which defied precise specification because it seemed to move in a dozen directions at once, and, within this ocean of untidy ambivalence, certain islands of precision—clearly defined particular objectives, such as the adoption of uniformities of personal appearance more tedious, because more self-consciously contrived, than those of the larger "straight" society, new mores, expectations, and belongings, especially in regard to race, politics, economics, war and peace. What was—and is—happening here, I believe, is, on the one hand, a struggle to escape classification and to elude categories in which one could be contained and explained into unimportance and, on the other, a seeking of self-classification as one of a recognizable group. The second goal is essential because the first, to the degree that it is achieved, defeats itself: we escape the computer's frightening capacity to reduce us and all we believe to a dull statistic at the price of an equally uncomfortable and anonymous isolation.

In association with the longing for significance are some other demands today: for social justice, for peace, and for a new political order in place of forms that are said to be neither efficient, humane, nor really democratic. In the struggle for these goals many persons are becoming aware of the political aspects of our culture as the *motion* of the social machine which grinds them small, and the reaction of some is to wish to bring the motion to a halt and to destroy the machine in the hope that something less impersonal may be found or invented to replace it. Others attempt to seize control and to change the direction of the motion so that the machine may achieve new ends without actually being destroyed. Others, again, fearful of the great changes that are proposed and with, perhaps, much more to lose if the present order of things were abandoned, try to protect their interests by excluding the malcontents from the organs of power. The consequence is a deepening polarization of society whose end, if it continue, can only be disintegration.

Nor is the field of ethics and morality particularly serene. Young people are sincerely disturbed and disenchanted by the considerable gap between the ideals that most older citizens publicly espouse and the actual standards by which our society operates. It is not easy to see how passively polite acquiescence in church on Sunday to the commandment to love (that is, to seek the authentic good of) our neighbor as we love ourselves can be consistent with economic competition. Further, many of the moral injunctions of their parents seem to today's children simply outside the scope of reason. People who have been told that premarital sex is to be avoided because it may produce an unwanted baby, or disease, or harm to the psyche of at least one partner wonder legitimately what is wrong with it when conception can be averted, disease controlled, and when neither partner takes the matter too seriously. The imposition of mores that cannot be defended reasonably is just another tool for the achievement of meaningless living and contributes to the loss of significance of those who are forbidden to devise their own moral standards.

Out of the unstable mood we have been describing come a few additional questions concerning man's potential. The first of these is about the individual's capacity for participation in political processes. An assumption at the base of democratic conviction is the ability of all free citizens, other than the obviously mentally inadequate, to share at least indirectly in the decision-making of the state. Today there are attacks on the viability of present forms of democracy from two directions. On the one hand it is argued that there is great disparity between individual abilities to make wise choices, and the mass of men need therefore to be protected from their own incompetence. One way to do this is to place the responsibility for government (and the election of the governing body) in the hands of a proven elite. On the other hand there is the complaint that the modes of representational democracy presently devised (even if they are held to deserve the name "democracy" at all) do not really permit the will of the majority to be expressed because the individual is too far removed from the moments of actual decision. In the United States, for example, we are often presented with the option of voting to nominate and then to elect to various offices one of several candidates, none of whom enjoys our confidence. Yet the machinery whereby a man becomes a candidate, especially for the highest offices in the land, seems so complex, expensive to operate, and out of popular control that there may be nothing effective to be done short of demolishing the present system altogether. The question here that concerns us at present is of the proper locus of authority and the capacity of men to be responsible. Can we, in fact, operate a democracy? At some time in the future improved methods of communication will make it possible for governments to elicit popular opinion and within a few hours to know accurately what most people want. Will this present us with ideal government, or would we be better governed by a handful of experts, or even a benevolent despot? Perhaps government of the people, for the people, by computer would be best of all—if we could trust the initial programmers!

Related to this is another question which has relevance for many of our social institutions, including those of education and welfare: admitting disparity of ability, what are man's rights and possibilities for self-determination? Our failure to reach clarity about this frustrates our efforts in many directions. For instance, the benevolent white liberal tends, in the United States, so to act that he betrays his unconscious conviction that it is up to him to achieve justice for the black community, and that it is he who must determine the legitimate mode of racial interaction within his country. Similarly, many well-intentioned people would so direct poverty relief programs that they demonstrate their actual belief that the poor are inherently incapable of designing a better condition for themselves, and must therefore be manipulated like pieces on a chessboard. But neither the black man nor the poor white are necessarily willing to be remade according to any plan other than their own, and even if they were, the question would remain of the real usefulness of any "new" order that is not fashioned and chosen by those who are to fill it. At least among the most sensitive people in the categories we are discussing it is the right and the means of self-determination that is eagerly desired; the removal of obstructions and the facilitating of this process is what must be sought.

Another aspect of our present concern is the problem of the individual's right of dissent. The war in Vietnam has made this issue critical for us, but it is equally vital in considerations of who shall determine moral codes for whom, what political and economic structure our nation shall have, and many other issues. Obviously, society cannot survive in the absence of a large consensus on many subjects, or without some ability to restrain the activities of the deviant. But it is equally obvious to most of us that there are limits to the conformity which the state may demand of us beyond which lies the enslavement of our mind and spirit.

Finally, many of us in this troubled time are suffering what we may call self-estrangement. This may express itself as un-certainty about our personal goals, about our identity, about our belonging, or it may take the form of a dislike of what we know ourselves to be, a dislike so serious that we are driven into a profoundly psychopathological state. The increasing sig-nificance of psychotherapists (who constitute a sort of secular priesthood) and the heavy burden of counseling which sym-pathetic clergymen are called upon to bear give testimony to our disenchantment with ourselves as well as to our bewilder-ment about the world.

Behind all these particular issues lie the questions: What are our human capacities to make our own decisions and live our own lives? What sort of political animal might we be? What can we realistically dream for ourselves and our society?

Clearly, men are unequal in ability and it is unlikely that they can be made equal by education, since there are well-informed and even scholarly fools, and the process of infusing or educing wisdom is one that eludes us. What, then, are the premises of a *humane* politics and social order which shall do the best that can be done with the diverse material comprising any community? And how shall we collectively enhance the potential for fulfillment of every individual?

Next, and connected closely with what has been said, we must raise a question about the nature of human community itself. We suffer today an obvious decay of that mutual care which builds community and from this lack emerges the grim rise of violence, crime, and mutual exploitation of labor and management, seller and buyer, parent and child, as well as the many other divisions of which we are becoming so explosively aware. If true community ever existed, how shall we recover it? If it did not, how shall we create it? It is necessary that we ask this not only about small, local communities but also about the larger and necessarily less intimate community of the world at large.

History offers us so little hope of tranquillity over long periods, and the present age is imperiled in so many ways that men grow weary and shallow of hope. The strongest empires have fallen, the most unified nations have suffered defeat, the world has erupted in blood and smoke so many times that young people today could surely be excused for devising a radical existentialism which valued only the discrete moments in their living presence and shunned consideration of the future. Is there, somewhere, a clue that might lead us to a recipe for peace? If there is not, can we find some basis for hope of a different sort? Can we find the means of valuing and living constructively in a world chronically in disarray?

GOD AND HUMAN EXPERIENCE

Partly as a result of factors we have already considered, God has become a problem for us. To put it briefly, the God of Christian belief seems as alien to human experience as an altruistic politician.

To begin with, there is a problem about the very word "God." What can it possibly mean? If, like Paul Tillich, we hold it to be the verbal symbol for the object of a man's "ultimate concern," it has a certain usefulness, of course, because it saves us the employment of several words whenever we wish to speak about that object in an abstract way. But men are likely to be ultimately concerned about various things, so that the meaning of the word changes from one person to the next. As soon as we try to ascend from the most general level of abstraction (to ask, for instance, what a man's most *ap-*

propriate ultimate concern is) we are likely to find ourselves soon bogged again in a miasma of ambiguity.

We may avoid some of the word's problems, of course, by beginning with certain assumptions. We may decide that the word shall have a specifically Christian meaning; that it will refer, for us, only to the proper Ultimate Concern of Christian men and women, and we may go farther and specify that this means the Creative Being who is the source of all conditioned beings; that he is characterized by love (as the New Testament declares) and is both immanent and transcendent inasmuch as there is no place where he is not, yet the vast sum of all places does not exhaust his being.

We need go no farther than this, however, to locate the basis of modern man's difficulty. There was a time when all men were, in some fashion, theologians or philosophers; there have been periods (the seventeenth century in England?) when it might almost be said that all men were poets. But today all men are scientists. We depend upon the observable, measurable thing or event and we have long forgotten that the word "mystery" has any meaning other than ignorance. So how can we deal with a nonempirical deity? The very possibility of such a phenomenon is so far beyond the temper of our minds that we cannot even really be interested in it for the sake of argument. It might even be said that until his existence can be confirmed in the strictest empirical manner and something learned about him that is measurable, he cannot even be spoken about.

But if all of us are, in some sense, scientists, it is nevertheless true that for many of us the comprehensive adequacy of science has been called into question by other moods and movements among us, chiefly existentialism. We have become aware that there are areas of life and concern where cold, dispassionate objectivity is irrelevant or worse. We know that there are truths which are found or forged only in the fires of the most deeply personal encounters. We know that what is really important about life and about man (or at least those men and women about whom we care most) can never be measured or understood by scientific method. But even knowing this, we look askance at God.

Our problem as existentialists is that existence is so ambiguous, so filled with an irrational blending of good and evil, so apparently meaningless and haunted by terrible shadows that it is not possible to think of the Christian God as having any part in it. If we lived in the "best of all possible worlds," we could believe in him, but the theodicy of Leibnitz sounds strange and strained to us now. We have drunk too deeply of the cup of suffering, and we have watched the twisting shapes of sorrow too long to escape hypocrisy when, in sentimental moments, we talk about the ultimate goodness of the will of God. No, if God is good, he is patently weak or stupid. If he is omnipotent, he is patently vicious. Faced with these alternatives, most of us prefer to be alone in the universe rather than to accept such company.

In *The Brothers Karamazov*, Fyodor Dostoevsky has Ivan speak about suffering:

> I want to be there when every one suddenly understands what it has all been for. All the religions of the world are built on this longing, and I am a believer. But then there are the children, and what am I to do about them? That's a question I can't answer.[4]

He concludes that the "higher harmony" which human suffering is supposed by some to serve is "not worth the tears of that one tortured child who beat itself on the breast with its little fist and prayed in its stinking outhouse, with its unexpiated tears, to 'dear kind God'!"[5]

Here is the crux of the matter for most of us. How can the undeserved suffering of the world be reconciled with belief in a just, merciful, and omnipotent God? A contemporary novelist has one of his characters put the matter succinctly:

> If the universe was made, it was made by an idiot, and an idiot crueler than Nero. There are no laws. Atoms and animals alike do only what they can't help doing.

Natural history is a study of horrible things. You say
you read the papers; but have you ever walked around
the skeleton of a brontosaurus? Or watched microbes
in a drop of water gobble each other up? [6]

Of course, one may argue that God is neither vicious nor
evil, but that he is embattled; that there are forces in the universe which he does not control. Edgar Sheffield Brightman, a
Christian philosopher, talked about what he called "the Given,"
a sort of recalcitrance in the universe with which God must
work, and Zoroastrianism pictured a cosmos that was the bat-
tleground of two warring spirits, one good and one malicious.
The heretical Christian scholar Marcion believed the world to
have been made evil by an evil God but redeemed by a good
one. And Norman Mailer, in *The Deer Park,* adds a new twist
when he seems to suggest that God has found himself so impotent to achieve good that he has turned to evil as a more satisfying way of exhibiting power.

But all these speculations seem idle to most of us. The essential facts are that God is intangible and that the world is
ambivalent. Given these two elements of our common experience, we find it hard to take seriously any claims for the
existence of such a God as Christians talk about. Where once
he guaranteed our dream, he now discomforts us at best and
is too shaky a foundation for our hope. Can he be replaced?
Can we ourselves take his place? The loss of him is part of the
trouble with our dream today.

CONCLUSION

We have so far attempted to outline some aspects of the
picture that man sees when he looks at the hazy reflection of
himself in the mirror of his time. We have seen that many of
the basic questions we ask ourselves now are the questions men
asked long before Socrates, but there is a difference of accent
because our time is new and newly perilous, and old answers
may no longer satisfy.

The question at the heart of all our searching of ourselves is this: What is man; what is his appropriate mode of being in the world; what is his destiny or ultimate possibility? But what we are asking here is not made clear until we see that within this question are some others: Is there any purpose to be discovered in the coming-to-be of the universe? With or without such a purpose, what is the possibility of freedom and self-determination and satisfaction for this human animal who is so clearly part of a continuum with the non-human? How is human life to be valued? By its economic productivity? its happiness? its length? What is the meaning of human power and achievement? Do these mean that we are today indeed in a "world come of age" in which there is no room and maybe no possibility of God? Is the individual significant, or only the society or state? What are the premises of human political structuring? What are defensible bases for human morality, and how can true community be established? Or is man better without community? Where shall we find peace, personal and social? Does the suffering and confusion of the world mean that it is essentially meaningless? Must it make its own meanings, or is there within or beyond it (or both) some Ground of meaning and of value, that is to say, a God?

If we should now try to gather all these questions into one, it might be this: Knowing, somehow, deeply within us that we are unfinished, and longing as men always have longed to become complete and to know our destiny and our fulfillment, where can we seek them? When we sink back for a moment from the mindless busyness of our days to let our spirits find renewal in a hope, where shall we find that fragile greenness? In a word, when the man of our time allows himself to dream, what dreams may come?

Part Two
BUDDHISM

II

Being, Truth, and Ignorance

Vain to expect
Tomorrow for the cherry.
—*Attributed to Shinran*

Before we begin an attempt to suggest a Buddhist answer
to the questions that were raised in Part One, a word of warning is in order. Buddhism, like Christianity, has been sufficiently
vigorous to provoke the arising of numerous sects and schools
of thought, and there is a wide range of disagreement among
these on various doctrinal and methodological points. At a
very remote time a major schism developed with several rela-
tively conservative sects on one side and a burgeoning group
of allegedly more liberal ones on the other; the latter called
themselves collectively the *Mahāyāna* ("Great Way" or "Great
Vehicle") and their opponents the *Hīnayāna* ("Lesser Way" or
Vehicle). Naturally these titles did not appeal strongly to the
fancy of the "*Hīnayāna*" schools, and since only one of them
survives in vigor in the present day, it seems better to avoid
the pejorative "*Hīnayāna*" in favor of the name of this specific
sect *Theravāda*—meaning the "Way of the Elders."

Of the *Mahāyāna* about a dozen sects survive today and of
these the strongest are those known in Japanese as the *Jodo
Shin Shu* ("True Pure Land Sect"), *Jodo Shu* ("Pure Land
Sect"), *Zen* ("Meditation"), *Shingon* ("True Word"), and

Nichiren (a distinctively Japanese school founded in the thirteenth century by an extraordinarily forceful individual named Nichiren). These sects are often themselves divided into subsects, so that the number of recognizable and institutionalized Buddhist groups rivals that of Christianity.

If we think of the distinction between *Theravāda* and *Mahāyāna* as similar in some respects to that between Roman Catholicism and Protestantism and then see that as Protestantism has given birth to various denominations which do not usually regard each other as "unchristian" but merely as failing to emphasize adequately some doctrinal or procedural option, we shall have at least a rough grasp of the situation in Buddhism (although *Nichiren*'s disavowal of other Buddhist groups has sometimes been excessively ungenerous!).

Sometimes the differences between two Buddhist groups are very small, and sometimes they reflect quite important divergences of philosophy; but in general it may be said that there is a broad central philosophy shared by most intelligent *Mahāyānists*, and largely from this we shall now fashion one of the possible responses which Buddhism may make to the question of man's dream.

We are impermanent. No matter how far science stretches our capacity for survival we shall remain mortal and fragile. It is with the acceptance of this fact that Buddhism begins its analysis of our human condition, for when one adds to it a second datum—that as wondrously self-conscious, self-valuing entities we have difficulty living contentedly a lifetime of reluctant farewells that ends in our own oblivion—one has the base for a profound understanding of what it means to be human.

A baby is at first, we may presume, without any discrimination of objects. Soon, however, consciousness begins to emerge and take shape, and at last a difference is perceived between that which moves more or less at his will, and that which does not but is instead a resistance of some sort. In other words, the baby begins, without verbalization, of course, to distinguish between the self and the not-self. It would be difficult to exaggerate the importance of this event, for the discovery of the distinction between "I" and "That," subject and object, is the foundation of our science (which with greater and greater precision explores the not-self), of our societal structures such as law and economics (which attempt to understand and regulate for the mutual safety of humans, and for their advantage, the relations of self and not-self), and, in some measure, of almost every common enterprise of mankind. It is this discrimination of self and other which provides the ground rules for the structures of our language and our logic, and it has so captured us that it is a rare man who ever imagines even dimly the possibility that we might think in some fashion other than in the dualistic way of separating self and the world of objects.

In short, the moment that we begin to discriminate between "myself" and other things or persons we set in motion a chain of experiences that produce a characteristically human way of thinking and of living. "I" become the valuing center of my universe, and all other things are valued in relation to me. "I" become capable of manipulating other entities, and of being manipulated. "I" become unique, stark, solitary—a center of consciousness and power, concerned with my own survival and success. All those things which are not myself can be friendly, neutral, or hostile, but their meaning is always really *their meaning for me.* And consequently I am vulnerable, capable of fear and shame. I can be attacked by every hostility to that which I have learned to call "mine." My reputation, my ambitions, my security, my beliefs, my life itself, are all open to assault.

It is this vulnerability of the discriminated self that Buddhism largely has in mind when it declares the first of its famous "Four Noble Truths": *To exist is to suffer.* "What now is the noble truth of suffering? Birth is suffering; decay is suffering; death is suffering; sorrow, lamentation, pain, grief, and

despair are suffering; not to get what one desires is suffering." [7]

As we indulge with increasing efficiency in the art of discrimination, we begin to take for granted that each discriminated thing is fully, finally, and irrevocably "real" without
qualification. "I" am a continuing, substantial, self-sustaining
center. Because I am finite and capable of sustaining loss, I
must protect myself, however, and this I can do by attaching
myself to enough objects of the right sort. That is, the more
objects of knowledge I possess, the stronger I am ("Knowledge
is power!"); the more material things I own, the greater is my
security; the more friends I have, the better am I able to participate in a corporate security ("A true friend is the best
possession," as a children's book of proverbs has it).

But the tragic weakness of this way of life lies in its basic
misunderstanding of reality. It presupposes that ours is an essentially stable, if not static, world and that change, loss, and
death are bizarre intruders. "I" am a consistent, enduring
entity, and so are all the other persons and things to which I
become attached, and it is therefore possible to protect ourselves from the aberrant appearance of decay, much as a person who is going to take a trip submits to vaccination in order
to avoid cholera. This, alas, is precisely *not* the truth. Rather,
the world as we experience it empirically is a constant flux.
Nothing endures, and there is nothing therefore that can lend
endurance to us.

> As stars, a fault of vision, as a lamp,
> A mock show, dew drops, or a bubble,
> A dream, a lightning flash, or cloud,
> So should one view what is conditioned. [8]

As the stars shine only when there is no sun in our sky, so the
world seems real only when we do not see the blazing Truth. In
fact, however, it is as ephemeral as dew, as fleeting as a
lightning flash, as insubstantial as a dream. So life is a succession of losses; disappointment follows disappointment, and even

our moments of elation and joy are prelude to other losses and new disenchantments. The mother who newly holds a baby in her arms dare not think how transitory is its life, but the fact is that we lose everything we love, or are lost to everything.

Thus, we suffer. To exist is to suffer. The Buddhist does not mean by this simply that we are victims of various particular pains, aches, and frustrations. These are only a part of the picture. He means, beyond these, that we walk always near shadows from which may lunge at any time the specter of our total and inescapable vulnerability. We suffer what the European existentialists have taught us to call *Angst*, "anxiety," an imprecise, often free-floating anxiety that may be hidden from our view (repressed, perhaps, because we are too timid to acknowledge it), but that cannot be utterly removed while we are finite beings with immortal longings, or at least longings for some sort of fulfillment.

Can we not understand, now, why developments in science in recent decades both elate and depress us? We are threatened by them when they call into question the self-sufficiency of our unique being, when they challenge our human pride by identifying us with chemical processes or something else that has no scent of the divine in it. We are proud and elated when science gives us a feeling of power to control our environment and our destiny. But the Buddhist wryly smiles at both our fear and our pride, knowing them to be but the opposite sides of a coin. They both express the conviction that our discrimination of ourselves as ultimately real, particular beings is a truth of absolute importance. If, for any reason, that "truth" is dispelled, then both the fear and the pride may become no more than pitiful irrelevancies.

What the Buddhist invites us to do, then, is to begin our thinking at a new place. However difficult this is, we must somehow put aside all the premises—conscious or unconscious —of our customary thought. As we shall see later, this may not be possible until we have undergone a certain remarkable experience, but we can point toward the possibility of a new perspective and simultaneously perhaps set the stage for the experience by trying to conceptualize the premises and main outline of a *Mahāyāna* philosophy.

> When the self dies, the universe flows in. If we can sense the meaning behind these tricks with words, we realize that egotistical notions block no-self. If we attain no-self, we become free from the opposites of "self and other" and experience oneness.[9]

Thus, in three sentences, the *Mahāyāna* Gospel is summarized. But we must probe for the meaning behind the words, and in doing so will at best only approximate what is intended.

Many Buddhists are fond of using the word "Suchness" (*Tathatā*). The suchness of things means their finally, absolutely authentic reality or essence. If the world were truly a collection of quite disparate things with no necessary connection between them—a genuine pluralism through and through —then to see the suchness of the world would be to see each thing in it as independent. It would be to see a flower as simply that particular flower, a tree as that particular tree, a man as that particular man. This is the way we ordinarily perceive things because of our unexamined premise that the world consists of this unique self and all those objects which surround it. But suppose that this way of seeing things is not wholly accurate; that it misses the ultimate truth about the world; that it is largely a habit and not a necessary way of understanding. Suppose that, while still noticing the flower and the tree and the man and perceiving them as these separate things, we could at the same time *see through their particularity* in such a way that (without canceling the particularity as one mode of their existence, albeit a secondary one) we see that at the deepest level of truth they are not separate. The suchness of the world, and of everything in it, then becomes an Ultimate Reality that is beyond distinctions and polarities, void (*śūnya*) of discriminations, of finitude, of any specifiable qualities which would enable us to talk about it with precision.

There are many words a Buddhist uses to name this Absolute
Reality, and each of them has its special usefulness. It is, for
example, *Bhūtatā* ("Reality"), *Satyatā* ("the True"), *Dhar-
madhātu* ("the Realm of Truth"), *Anutpāda* ("the Unborn"),
Dharmakāya ("the Body of Truth"), *Citta-mātra* ("Mind
Only"), and so on. But perhaps the most apt of all the possible synonyms is *Śūnyatā,* which means "the Void," implying
not that Reality is empty or nonexistent, but that it is devoid
of limiting qualities. It is beyond the discriminating intellect's
categories of definition.

The great danger, for the Westerner at least, in thinking
about *Śūnyatā* is that he will conceive of it as some great Thing
beside or behind all the other lesser things of the universe.
Nothing could be farther from the truth. Rather, *Śūnyatā* is
the reality, the suchness of all that is; it cannot be abstracted
from the everyday world of things, and they could not *be* if
their reality were not *Śūnyatā.*

There are flavors of Kant, Hegel, and Spinoza in all of this,
to be sure, but since the Buddhist does not come to his understanding through these philosophers it is better for us, if
we wish to approach an understanding of what is being said
here, to try to put Western philosophy away from us. Later,
when and if we have understood, we may enjoy the game of
comparisons, but for now it is important to concentrate on one
single line of thought and to leave the enticing byways for
another day.

We have, then, an Absolute which is the reality of every
existent. The immediate questions are: How does one come to
know this Absolute? What is its relation to particularity? What
is the relevance of this concept for our modern living?

The discovery of the Absolute is attained in an experience
that is variously called "enlightenment," "awakening," or (a
Japanese word made familiar by Zen) *satori.* What happens in
such an experience is that at last our familiar but false ways of
seeing the world drop away from us, our persistent, habitual
polarizing of reality into subject and object, self and other, this

and that, falls from us and in a moment of strange clarity we *see* the Truth. We know with an intense immediacy the Absolute which has hitherto lain disguised behind the masks and antics of the world. What we have now attained may be called *prajñā* ("wisdom") or *prajñāpāramitā* ("the wisdom that goes beyond," or "transcendental wisdom"), but the fact is that we have the greatest difficulty now in describing what has happened to us in the terms of conventional logic. We begin to say, "I perceive the vast Oneness which is the Truth of everything." But this will not do, for what we perceived utterly transcended the distinction between the perceiving "I" and the "Oneness" and the "everything." It was suddenly the case that "I" and "Oneness" and "everything" and even the act of perceiving were not to be separated. In one sense each truly was, but most deeply all were simply One. How does one describe this without doing violence to language? Perhaps poetry is the form of speech most nearly adequate for our purpose. There is an old Chinese poem that may be translated:

> A bird gives a cry—
> The mountains quiet all the more.

Yoshinori Takeuchi comments:

> The voice is felt first as disturbing; then, by contrast,
> the first stillness is recollected; and by integrating all
> three moments of stillness, voice, and stillness into one
> single impression, a deepened feeling of stillness pre-
> vails in the listener's mind. The voice of the bird be-
> comes the voice of the Stillness itself.[10]

The bird's cry is, thus, analogous to particular things in the world. It *is*, indeed, a thing-in-itself; yet it may be experienced as the surrounding and encompassing Stillness giving voice to itself, so that the Stillness is present in the cry. The Stillness *is* the cry; yet the cry is not to be naïvely identified with the Stillness.

Alas, we have failed again. At best the curtain of obscurity may, for someone, have been shaken a little and an instant of light may have escaped, but the expressing of the experience of awakening to Truth eludes us still. One thing is certain. Our new perception was not gained by a process of deliberate rationality. We have broken out of the furrows of logical process and have seen something for which rationality itself is never prepared. There was a "dawning," a moment when our whole being cried out, "Ah!" with delight and astonishment. And then, as we turned to tell our friends about our discovery, we found that such an experience cannot be translated into words. We can only point in a direction; we can circle around the experience, as near as words will let us come. But no matter what we say, until the light flashes for him, no one will see what we have seen.

We encounter the Absolute, then, intuitively rather than rationally, but perhaps we can build a springboard for intuition, and this is what we shall try to do as we continue to speak about the indescribable and unnameable.

The truth is not, ultimately, pluralism but Absolutism. Very well, but this is no simple monist Absolute we point to which would enable us to say that all that we meet day by day is illusion, completely unreal. Things are. How, then, does the Absolute relate to the particular things of our experience? Our poem about the bird's cry was one attempt to specify this, but is there any other way in which we can approach the question?

One way of trying to approximate an answer, although a rough one, is to speak as if there were two levels of suchness, or two dimensions of the Absolute: the conditional and the unconditional. The latter is, so to speak, the Absolute as it is in itself, unimaginable, undivided, transcending all qualifications. The former is the universe as we see it. Conditioned suchness is, thus, suchness speaking to us and appearing in terms that our fogbound, pluralizing mind can grasp. This means that the Absolute viewed through the spectacles of our categorizing intelligence appears as the pluralistic world; the world, seen after we have taken off those spectacles, is the Absolute.

Another approach to our question may be made by speaking of the particular things in the world as "expressions" or "manifestations" of the Absolute. The Absolute is beyond birth and death, yet all that is born is its self-expression. In a grain of wheat we actually see the Absolute affirming itself; in a baby's first cry we hear its "lion's roar." Every particular thing is the great "I Am" of Ultimate Reality.

Yet this is not wholly satisfactory, either, because to speak of things as the self-expression or the manifestation of Śūnyatā may suggest that Śūnyatā is some tangible substance which crops up in various shapes. Instead, the truth is that particularity really exists, even though all particular things are transient, but that all particular, transitory existence is finally none other than Śūnyatā; yet Śūnyatā is not divided. However this fractures logic, we have to say at once both that particularity exists and that nevertheless one thing is real: Śūnyatā.

It must be clear by now that every set of terms in which we try to embrace the Buddhist Absolute turns out to be no more than metaphor, so we may as well resort to a little overt picture-thinking which has been honored by time and use. Legend tells of a net owned by the great god Indra. It was unique in that it was made of highly reflective gems, and the wonderful effect of this was that when one gazed at a single gem one could see at once that isolated stone in its beautiful particularity and, reflected in it, the entire net. What, then, would one say was the truth about what could be seen? Did truth lie with the singular or with the All? Both, and neither without the other. But whereas European existentialism would say that the existent (the single gem) was prior to the essence (the net), Buddhism reverses this and says that what we discover in the illuminating moment of *satori* is that it is more nearly true to say that the Absolute melts itself into particularity than that particularity stands alone or even coalesces to produce the Absolute.

It is worth noting that all that we have said applies as much to Time as it does to Space or to entities that exist in time and are extended in space. Thus, although we commonly experience time as a succession of moments, the profounder truth is that each moment is itself eternity. Each moment is a fleeting instant, yet each is also Absolute.

This has several interesting implications which we shall merely point to at present. First, my life is, as it were, wholly present in every moment. I am, as I write this, fully alive and completely dying. What I am is conditioned or determined by past experiences and decisions—but the moment comprehends every past instant and I am therefore not bound, but freely self-determining now. Secondly, the Buddhist view of history is different from the typical Western one which has been shaped by the traditions of Judaism and Christianity, for it is not linear, as theirs is, teleological, aiming toward the fulfillment of a divine intention. Especially it has no "central" moment or event, no exodus and no Christ-event which gives meaning to the whole. For the Buddhist, there is no particular beginning or end, and no center, for each moment is the fullness of Śūnyatā just as each flower is the entire universe, and no moment looks to another for its justification or its meaning.

Here, then, is the basis for Mahāyāna speculation about life and the true meaning of the events in life. The individual person or thing or moment is marked by transience and doomed to pass, yet this is true only insofar as it is thought of as individual, as self-authenticating and self-existent. As soon as we see in it not only this particular but also the universal, it becomes eternal.

Because many Western readers will find our discussion so far somewhat alien (and therefore more unpersuasive than the ideas deserve to be), and being justified by the fact that it is a sound Buddhist technique to approach the rationally unattainable Truth by a variety of paths, I shall now, more briefly, try to recapitulate the chief ideas of this chapter, using a few new symbols.

Mahāyāna Buddhism teaches that the fears, anxieties, sufferings, and maladies of life originate in delusion. Intellectually, this delusion is essentially the failure to see the emptiness (*śūnyatā*) of things or that their "suchness" (*tathatā*), their final reality, is not their existential particularity but a ubiquitous and eternally undivided Ground which may variously be called the Void, the Buddha-Mind, the Buddha-Nature, the Unborn, or (in Western parlance) the Absolute. It is neither personal nor impersonal in itself, but it is nothing else than this which we perceive in every personal and impersonal phenomenon. Emotionally, our delusion expresses itself chiefly as desire, a thirst for things, experiences, attainments, and immortality.

Our desire continues to obscure our vision, so that we do not apprehend the Truth, because it attaches us to particular objects as though they were themselves completely real and adequate, basically other than us and therefore eligible to be sought and acquired.

In our loss of the perception of the Void and our conviction that particular things are finally real, we come to believe in the separate, isolated reality of some enduring self within us for which we plan and hope great things. Alas, we are frustrated in our hoping because all through our lives our hopes are incompletely attained or, if fulfilled, strangely unsatisfying after all. And at the end there awaits us death, which is the final crushing absurdity to mock our building and acquiring.

We come, then, to think of death as the last enemy. But it is more important to see birth as the *first* enemy. To be born as a man is to be born into the practice of discrimination which falsely particularizes Reality, and our problem therefore is not somehow to survive death but somehow to overcome birth!

> This is where Buddhism offers us its good news: The human mind possesses the Buddha-nature unobtainable from others. It can be compared with a man who has a jewel in his clothes which he knows not of, or to a man who seeks after food when he has a treasure in his own storehouse.[11]

In other words, our ignorance of the presence of the Buddha-Nature in every being and our searching frantically for meaning, value, and salvation in a hundred different places are the pitiful accompaniments of delusion. Our joyful deliverance comes when we stop looking in the wrong places for a meaning and an immortality that were always in us, "hidden" behind the masks of error. The Buddha-Nature is none other than *Sūnyatā,* the eternal Void. It is not subject to birth or death; it is beyond lust and loss, for there is nothing it is not. The great Japanese Buddhist master, Dogen, expresses this idea with typical subtlety:

> Hearing the raindrops from the eaves,
> Here am I, empty, with no-mind:
> The raindrops sound: that is,
> The raindrops hear themselves.[12]

The last lines of this short verse could be translated: "The raindrops now are no other than myself." The Absolute is being affirmed here and it transcends but embraces both the hearer and the heard.

We shall conclude this chapter with a warning and two observations. Someone who has struggled through the admittedly elusive speculation above might conclude that we have been saying that the Ultimate Reality is undivided and eternal, but that it expresses itself in the world so that each item of mundane existence is a piece of this Reality. This would be a serious misunderstanding. The truth is more difficult than that to comprehend. Each particular thing or person *is* the Absolute; *Sūnyatā* is wholly present, for it cannot be divided. This means (O poor, long-suffering logic!) that the Absolute in you faces the Absolute in me, and our relationship can best be described as an "interpenetration of Absolutes." This logically curious phrase was used by D. T. Suzuki, and apparently derived by him from an important Buddhist work, the *Gandavyūha,* of which he wrote:

> The ruling idea of the *Gandavyūha* is known as the doctrine of interpenetration. . . . Each individual reality, besides being itself, reflects in it something of

the universal, and at the same time it is itself because of other individuals. A system of perfect relationship exists among individual existences and also between individuals and universals.[13]

So much for the warning. The first of our two observations is that among the many questions which all this must leave unresolved, the one most nagging to many Westerners is: If *Śūnyatā* is the Truth, how can the illusion arise in each of us that we are separate, fully independent selves? Can the Absolute be self-deceived? It must be admitted that *Mahāyāna* philosophers have not been clear about this and have usually not even attempted an answer. A modern Zen thinker of Western background, Beatrice L. Suzuki, comments simply that "mentation somehow moves in the wrong direction, and there is the rising of thoughts whereby the world is perceived in all its multitudinousness." [14] Sometimes it is pointed out that Asvaghosa has said that the illusion is a spark of consciousness that spontaneously flashes from the depths of suchness. This would seem to mean that our consciousness is inseparable from the ignorance that is our problem, and it is certainly true that to be conscious is very soon to begin to discriminate subject and object. But these are not really answers to our question.

Eliot Deutsch argues that for *Vedānta* the question of the origin of ignorance and its locus cannot even be intelligibly asked, for when one has realized Ultimate Reality (*Brahman* in the *Vedānta* system, *Śūnyatā* in the *Mahāyāna*) there is no ignorance to discuss, and until one reaches this happy state "one cannot establish a temporal origin to that which is conceivable only in time . . . or describe the process by which this ignorance ontologically comes to be." [15] This would, I think, be a line of reasoning acceptable to *Mahāyāna* Buddhists who, however, are likely, following Buddha's example in such matters, simply to classify the whole issue as an unprofitable question and bid us to seek that state of enlightenment in which the problem itself disappears.

The second observation is this: We have defied logic in

various places in our discussion so far, and this is not necessarily damning, for logic may well be a more arbitrary fiction
than we usually assume. But neither is our cavalier slashing of
logic a proof of profundity, truth, or superiority to some more
amenable system of thought. The authentication of *Mahāyāna*
must lie elsewhere, and for most adherents it lies in the profound experience of enlightenment. If what we have said above
serves reasonably well to specify what one learns when enlightened, and if it prepares the ground for the great awakening to occur, then it is justified. Otherwise, it is empty speculation and a futile torrent of words. But the skeptical Westerner,
moving in the murky atmosphere of psychological analysis with
which his culture is so fecund, wants to know how the experience itself is authenticated: subjectivity, he says, is a grossly
unreliable guide to truth. Here he meets the enigmatic smile of
the Buddha. If you have had the experience, you *know* it is
true; it is its own authentication, even if (as William James
observed) it can be so only to one who has had it.

Earlier we asked three questions: How does one know the
Absolute? What is its relation to particularity? What is the
relevance of our understanding of the Absolute for modern
living? Only the last question remains to be answered, and that
answer is the subject of the next chapters.

III
Buddhist "Being in the World"

No more worry about your not being perfect!
—*From "On Believing in Mind"*

Buddhaghosa, a fifth-century *Theravādin* monk, tried to explain the Buddhist notion of the lack of ego with these words:

> The monk, when he moves forwards or backwards, is not like a blind worldling who in his delusion thinks that it is a self which moves, or that the movement has been produced by a self, as when one says, "I go forwards," or "the act of going forwards is produced by me." But, free from delusion, he thinks: "when there arises in the mind the idea 'I will move forward,' then there arises also . . . a nervous impulse which originates from the mind and generates bodily expression." It is thus that this heap of bones, which is politely called a "body," moves. . . . Who then is the one who walks? To whom does this walking belong? In the ultimate sense it is the going of impersonal physical processes.[16]

Mahāyāna Buddhism, however, carried its thinking a step farther, into Absolutism, and maintains that what, in Buddhaghosa's anecdote, goes forward is ultimately *Śūnyatā*, which is neither personal nor impersonal, neither one nor many, but is beyond all signification. And *you* are not other than this indefinable Ultimate.

Consequently, a man's highest privilege and possibility, as well as his greatest need, is to discover for himself his continuity with Absolute Truth, with Reality which is imperishable. This discovery is, as we have seen, not the learning of a proposition, but the immersion in an experience in which "I" and "Thou" and "It" are overcome in the immediate perception of That which each of them is. When this discovery is made, there follow some striking implications for our daily life.

The first thing for us to notice is the way in which virtually all the disturbing new facts that confuse contemporary man's self-image are rendered harmless by *Mahāyāna* Absolutism. Whether we are thinking about organ transplants, the psychological manipulation of the masses by an elite, genetic engineering, the origin of the human species, the precarious value of the individual, or the inevitability of death itself, a new meaning suffuses everything when the world is viewed through the spectacles of Buddhist enlightenment. The decisive fact is that *Śūnyatā* ultimately bears all things and is disturbed by none. But for the sake of clarity we must pursue this idea a little further.

When we are anxious, the thing that is being threatened is our self and that to which we attach the self. It is true, of course, that in the sweeping tides of this industrial era there are plenty of dangers. As we have already seen, for example, the growing use of sophisticated computers may eventually make each of us an open book to authorities who wish it so, and the possibility of brain transplants raises the question of *who* survives, and of whether anyone is more than a set of interchangeable organs. Biochemistry seems to represent us as mere chemical syntheses or processes, and the various determinisms of social science rob us of tragedy and leave us pathetic units of a process whose power we usually do not even recognize. When our self-esteem comes face-to-face with such realities as these, we know ourselves to be embattled and long for a piece of solid ground on which to stand and declare ourselves to be unique, irreducible, unrepeatable selves with a certain intrinsic value.

But you must die, and so must I. And in the meantime all the glory that we thought we were trailing through our little moment of time is being steadily eroded. Well, this little self of which I am so protective—what is it really? Is it not a flickering instance of the Ultimately Real? My reality is not the name my parents gave me or the body they fashioned: I *am* my parents! I am also my children! I am that Eternity of which all these are mere moments, and I am a moment of that Eternity which each of them is. I am that which threatens and that which is threatened, victor and victim, the beginning and the end. My reality is that of the Absolute which is not and cannot be harmed or distorted by what occurs within it.

This does not mean, as a more simple monism would, that my apparent individuality as my "self" is quite unreal and illusory. As the man who sits at a typewriter now I am real enough and probably less enduring (at any rate more susceptible to colds) than my keyboard. But when I break through my finite self-consciousness I know that it is also true that he who was born in a certain Australian town with a ridiculous name over forty years ago is also and forever the Unborn! So of what could I possibly be afraid? What could I want that I have not, and am not, already? The little shape of truth that walks in these clothes and bears this name may be hungry and cold and poor, but the Truth is rich and full with an irrepressible fullness, and I am the Truth.

The processes of the world, which include the works of human ingenuity and human maliciousness, are *Śūnyatā,* and there are therefore in final Truth no wounds to bleed and no death to endure.

Now, all this might conceivably lead me to a mood of indifference to the world, and there can be no doubt that this has sometimes been the result of the kind of thinking we have outlined above. But as a good *Mahāyānist* I find myself drawn to an attitude that is not so simple or so irresponsible. If *Śūnyatā* is the great womb which, giving birth to all, *is* all, it is nevertheless true that this "all" and every particular which it embraces has its sphere of value and, as we shall see in due course, there are ethical demands which must be met. At the moment, however, let us fix in our minds one great idea: Because the final Truth is not a simple pluralism, and individual finitude is not the whole description of our state, my vulnerability as a person is not the threat it seemed to be:

> In the higher realms of true Suchness
> There is neither self nor other.
> When direct identification is sought,
> We can only say, Not two.
> One in all,
> All in one—
> If only this is realized,
> No more worry about your not being perfect![17]

In short, as a human being who has been born, I will laugh and cry, live, love, and die. But as eternally the Unborn I am beyond the hopeless limitation of "myself."

At the same time, the sense of elation, of power, and of limitlessness that often comes to modern Western man because of his remarkable technical achievements is exposed by Buddhism as so much froth and bubble. Man is, to borrow the title of a delightful contemporary fantasy, a mouse that roars, but to ears other than his own the roar is ridiculously like a squeak, after all. Our feelings of expansiveness and pride arise from the mistaken idea that as so many independent egos we have combined to transcend nature and to master it. We are capable of walking on the moon, and it seems to us that this is a godlike accomplishment. But if Buddhism comforts the frightened man by pointing to the ineffable glory of his essential reality, it brings the proud man down by saying that whatever he accomplishes in the role he plays as Man is, from the perspective of Truth, a trifle and a link in the chain that binds him to illusion. In short, we are confronted here with a perspective that reveals what may seem to be a kind of paradox: while we understand ourselves as essentially or exclusively these particular egos, the greatest things we do are like the games of children; but understand yourself truly through the apprehension of *Śūnyatā* and your lightest act becomes a miracle of mystery and simple grandeur:

> Miraculous! How wonderful!
> I draw water, I carry wood![18]

For the *Mahāyānist*, the problems of personal identity and of value assume a different shape. It is of no consequence that the idea that we are the specially favored creatures of a personal God becomes difficult to defend, for this is no part of Buddhist thought anyway. Nor can the universe ever become so vast that we are humiliated and discomforted by our corresponding insignificance. Our being has, as it were, two levels: as a particular human individual we are transient. But since there is no discontinuity between a man and the infinite Ground of his being, his reality is that of the universe and nothing can diminish him.

Nor should the Buddhist be entrapped in the anxious quest for personal "identity" or significance that colors the adolescence of Westerners. The important question is not concerned with *who* you are, but *what* you are, and when, in enlightenment, you can make the "lion's roar" of affirmation of yourself as absolute, there is indeed "no more worry about your not being perfect."

Essentially, then, Buddhism presents a very positive and even cheerful response to the question, "What is man?" What becomes, however, of the problem of human evil? If the *Śūnyatā* doctrine is true, how can we account for the malicious assaults that men inflict upon each other, the insidious manipulations of each other, the destructive and disgusting elements of human behavior? The greatest of all Japanese Buddhist thinkers, Dogen Kigen, offers the following:

> Concerning the problem of . . . evil, three kinds of disposition may be distinguished [of mind]: the good, the evil, and the indifferent. The evil is one of them.

Nevertheless, the evil disposition is in its very nature
birthless; the good and the indifferent also are birthless.
All are birthless, immaculate and finally real.[19]

What seems to be intended by this rather characteristically
difficult paragraph of Dogen's is the idea that the Unborn,
Śūnyatā, is the reality of all that exists, and consequently when
a mind turns to evil, even that by which and with which it
does so (its energies and so on) is the Unborn. Not only the
good, but even the evil disposition is birthless and in its essential nature "immaculate." It is only the form it takes in the
empirical world that can be called "evil."

There is, then, no *substantial* entity of evil; there are only
actual manifestations of the Absolute which bear the temporal
shape of evil. But why does even this form of evil exist in a
world whose Ultimate Reality is the Absolute?

The answer to this is contained in the Buddhist idea that the
condition of unenlightenment is one of ignorance and delusion.
As Socrates might have said, no man does evil knowing it to
be harmful to himself; he does it because he thinks it somehow
produces his good. Ignorantly, he does not know that one cannot harm another without doing the harm to oneself because
the "other" is not finally other at all. The answer, then, to the
problem of crime and human viciousness, as well as to all forms
of human anxiety and frustration, is that awakening to Truth
which is called enlightenment.

But even this does not really remove all the problems that
the presence of evil introduces to our discussion. Even if evil
can finally be reduced to ignorance (and let us admit that not
everyone will be persuaded of this), how does ignorance arise
within Śūnyatā? What is it that is in the state of delusion?
Does not logic force us to say that the Absolute is the seat and
victim of all error? But how can the Absolute be deceived?

The problem of evil, thus, resolves itself into the problem of
illusion—of the "going astray" of mentation—which we discussed in our last chapter, and there are few explicit attempts
to deal with it in Buddhist philosophy. Generally the *Mahā-*

yānist response would be to point out that this is an unanswerable, and therefore unprofitable, question. The *arising* of evil is a fact, however it occurred. The *overcoming* of it is what concerns Buddhism. You do not need to know how, where, and from whom you caught measles before remedial steps can be taken. An earnest man named Māluñkyāputta once demanded that the Buddha answer a series of questions before he, Māluñkyāputta, would become a follower, and the Buddha's reply is as relevant (or irrelevant) for our questions about the locus of evil and ignorance as it is for Māluñkyāputta's:

> It is as if, Māluñkyāputta, a man had been wounded by an arrow thickly smeared with poison, and his friends and companions, his relatives and kinsfolk, were to procure for him a physician or surgeon; and the sick man were to say, "I will not have this arrow taken out until I have learnt whether the man who wounded me belonged to the warrior caste, or to the Brahman caste, or to the agricultural caste, or to the menial caste." . . . Or again he were to say, "I will not have this arrow taken out until I have learnt whether the arrow which wounded me was an ordinary arrow, or a claw-headed arrow, or a vekaṇḍa, or an iron arrow, or a calf-tooth arrow, or a karavīrapatta." That man would die, Māluñkyāputta, without ever having learnt this.[20]

We are left, then, with a magnificent prospect for man. But this can become my Truth not by mere intellectual assent to a doctrine, but through an experience in which I *become* the unity of my particularity with the Absolute. Not until I am ready to forsake the priorities of my little ego and all that it claims as its own can I know the transcendence of that ego and enter the Truth. When that happens, I am indeed a new man, and the whole world is renewed in my eyes. I must still live out my life with the usual physical limitations, but in comprehension I know and am become the Truth that excludes nothing, and I am therefore radically and deeply free. But note once more: This is not a kind of monism in which my particularity becomes unreal and melts away into the Absolute. Rather, what I now know is that the Absolute melts into my particularity, and into all other particular existents, without being diminished or divided. A plague on logic!

What, in a scheme of thought such as we have been examining is man's proper mode of being in the world?

There have been philosophers who strenuously denied that "Man" and "the world" were two real and separate entities whose relationship one could meaningfully discuss. Thoroughgoing monists, they have tried to make every experience of dualism or pluralism a mere illusion, and have found their comfort in an unbroken and unmoving One. It is not easy to see why, if one takes this position, one does not immediately relapse into eternal silence, for to whom could one talk? (I am reminded of the friend of Bertrand Russell who told him that she had discovered in solipsism the perfect solution to all the philosophical problems of life, and only wondered why everybody else did not accept it too.)

There have been others who argued for a dualism or pluralism of realities despite the fact that there seems to be an innate longing in most of us for the neatness of simplicity.

Mahāyāna faces the question of whether a man is other than his world and says both (and neither!) yes and no. Each man, every episode and entity, is *Śūnyatā;* therefore each exists— yet nothing exists except *Śūnyatā.* Otherness is part of our everyday experience. I look at you and know that your actions, your thoughts, your feelings, your moods are not mine. Yet when illumination comes to me I break through the illusory bonds of my petty selfhood and affirm myself as the Absolute —and paradoxically at the same time affirm *you* as absolute. Henceforth I know our encounter and relationship to be, not the casual engagement of two transiencies, but, to repeat a phrase used earlier, an "interpenetration of Absolutes."

Such a position inevitably leads to a discussion of our place and role in the world, but it is a discussion that is constantly

trembling on the brink of logical disaster, and not infrequently
falls headlong over the edge. The discomforting thing to
logicians, however, is the fact that the Buddhist seems to enjoy
the fall. He knows very well what he is to be in the world, and
if the description of his situation offends logic, that is logic's
problem, not his. This is nowhere better illustrated than in the
attitude which a *bodhisattva*, a *Mahāyāna* saint of true insight,
is supposed to adopt toward all other sentient creatures:

> The Lord said: Here, Subhuti, someone who has set
> out in the vehicle of a Bodhisattva should produce a
> thought in this manner: "As many beings as there are
> in the universe of beings, comprehended under the
> term 'beings'—egg-born, born from a womb, moisture-
> born, or miraculously born; with or without form; with
> perception, without perception, and with neither per-
> ception nor non-perception—as far as any conceivable
> form of beings is conceived: all these I must lead to
> Nirvāna, into that Realm of Nirvāna which leaves
> nothing behind. *And yet, although innumerable beings
> have thus been led to Nirvāna, no being at all has been
> led to Nirvāna.*" [21]

Heinrich Dumoulin expresses the same idea: "Though aware
of the nothingness of all things and of the ultimate irrelevance
of all exertions of the spirit, he never ceases to work for the
benefit of all sentient beings." [22]

The root of this "logic of contradiction," as Dumoulin calls
it, lies, as we have seen, in the distinctive *Mahāyāna* notion
of the Absolute which is One and yet not One, which is Many
and yet not Many. Out of this arise two great central "qualities"
of the enlightened life, the marks of the *bodhisattva*, neither
of which can be absent or even modified, yet which are, in an
important sense, in irresolvable conflict: *karunā* and *prajñā*.

Karunā and *prajñā* together constitute an analysis of the
Mahāyāna "mode of being in the world" at its highest and are
thus the seeds out of which ethical and political theory and behavior must grow. What, then, do these words mean?

Karunā means "compassion," or even "love." The *Mahāyāna* saint exemplifies love because he knows that the suffering of one man is the suffering of all, and that no man's enlightenment can be complete until every man is enlightened. After all, how could it be otherwise when, in the doctrine of *Śūnyatā*, we are seen as not essentially separate? The *Mahāyāna* ideal, then, is not the ascetic who, attaining his own salvation, slips quietly from the human scene into some passionless peace, but of the *bodhisattva* who vows that he will not accept his ultimate release from the world and its troubles until all sentient beings are also released. So the *Mahāyānist* finds a rationale for social involvement, for activism in politics and ethics.

Prajñā means "wisdom" and in a *Mahāyānist* context is usually a synonym for *prajñāpāramitā,* the "wisdom that goes beyond," or "transcendental wisdom"—that is, ultimate wisdom about ultimate things. The *bodhisattva's* very nature is a compound of *karunā* and *prajñā,* but what makes this a somewhat disorderly idea is the fact that the essence of *prajñā* is the understanding that despite the apparent multiplicity of the world's content, there is fundamentally "not two." So the *bodhisattva* never ceases to love all others—and knows that essentially there are no others. Or rather, there are others and yet there are not. The good *Mahāyānist* is devoted to the assistance of his fellows because *Śūnyatā* is all!

The coexistence of the apparent contradictories *karunā* and *prajñā* as the wellsprings of *Mahāyāna* effort produces the view that the ultimate value in life is the universalizing of *satori,* or enlightenment. All things and actions should, ideally, serve this end in some way, for the ills that haunt us can never be finally removed until all illusion is dispelled and Truth alone remains. This would be the state of the perfect realization of *prajñā* and it is to this end that *karunā* preeminently addresses itself.

Having thus specified the theoretical basis upon which the *Mahāyāna* mode of being in the world should be designed, let us turn to a consideration of some practical implications.

IV

Buddhist Man in His Society and the Natural Order

An ass looks into the well;
The well looks into the ass.

—*Zen saying*

Mahāyāna Buddhism is a luxuriant philosophical garden in which the seed sown by the Buddha two and a half millennia ago has flourished exquisitely and exotically. But is it practical? Is it simply a Japanese teahouse religion, elegant, subtle, and irrelevantly beautiful, or is it a religion for the street? How does—or should—it affect the daily life of the devotee?

When one has accepted *Mahāyāna,* one is committed to the idea that Buddhist enlightenment, with all that it entails of deliverance from the misunderstandings, false values, anxieties, and ambitions of the world, is the primary goal of life. This being so, a Buddhist must also be dedicated to the hope and task of extending enlightenment with its benefits to all sentient creatures. This means that, as a *Mahāyānist,* I must look upon the world without cynicism or despair, but with compassion, and my life should become a vehicle of the Truth. The formula for proper living is: *karunā* in the service of *prajñā;* love that will do whatever it must to awaken men to wisdom.

From this it follows that Buddhist ethics sees as merely means some things which would in certain other systems of thought be regarded as ends in themselves. The relief of poverty—and, equally, deliverance from excessive wealth perhaps —as well as the abolition of oppression and injustice, the establishment of a healthy social and political order, must all serve the end of the universalizing of enlightenment. A single ultimate objective thus draws all other aims into its service and imposes an order, a coherence, an intelligible hierarchy of values, upon all our efforts. Furthermore, because of this single dominating goal, things may sometimes have to be done which would, were they ends in themselves, probably be regarded in most societies as unacceptable.

That is to say, love which means to produce understanding may sometimes make use of methods that seem bizarre until it is realized that they most effectively serve love's purposes. It may even be that a calculated use of violence will be love's instrument, and cruelty may express compassion. So a Zen master, aware that a cherished student cannot quite make the leap into the suprarational sphere of Truth because he is bogged down in conventionalism and rationality, may suddenly strike the student or even twist his nose, not to relieve the master's own feelings of disgust, but in the hope that the unexpected act and flash of pain may be the "push" necessary to awaken the man to that Truth which is always missed in conventional ways of thinking and responding. A good example of cruelty aimed at breaking men open to the Truth is contained in a story allegedly told by Dogen but, in any case, a well-known part of the Zen tradition:

> Once [Nanchuan's] students, divided into two factions, were quarreling over a cat. Nanchuan suddenly took hold of it and said, "Boil down your contention to one word. If you can do so, I will not cut this cat in half but, if you cannot, I will." None of them could answer so he cut it in two with one stroke.[23]

What Nanchuan is trying to do here is to show that his students are engaged in an essentially meaningless dispute. When Truth is realized, there *is* only "one word" and the cat (which, incidentally, is not simply a cat but simultaneously the in-divisible Absolute) can only be cut in two so long as it is seen superficially as no more than flesh, bones, and fur. If they realized the undivided wholeness of the Truth, they would realize, too, that their dispute arose because of a spurious dichotomizing of "truth" and "error"; it was they who had already cut the "cat" of Truth in two, though they could do so only at the illusion-bound level of their prejudice and not in its character as Ultimate Reality.

Nanchuan's love, then, and his consequent striving to uni-versalize enlightenment even justifies an act of manifest cruelty through which the Truth may express itself (at least one of Nanchuan's disciples is reported to have attained instant en-lightenment as a result of hearing about this curious episode).

Love seeking to awaken wisdom: here is the root of the proper motive for the everyday life of the Buddhist. Although there is not space in the present book for a detailed explora-tion of all that this may mean, some implications can be briefly and, I hope, clearly drawn, and some of the *Mahāyānist's* pos-sible responses to the questions and problems that haunt our day may be demonstrated. I shall not attempt to be systematic, but merely to select for discussion topics that seem to have some illustrative merit.

The cluster of problems that arise from automation are directly addressed by Buddhist values. Can men who face a great deal of leisure be saved from boredom? Can they be delivered from destroying themselves and others? When there is little connection between a man's activities and his income, can he escape a sense of worthlessness, irrelevance, or even guilt?

Part of our problem lies in the fact that values which were once instrumental and relative tend at last to be made absolute. To work hard and productively is a virtue when oneself and others can be supported only in this way, but when a piece of work is not needed, it may be meaningless and without merit. If "the dignity of labor" were an absolute value, a squirrel in his treadmill would be more dignified than any of us. From a Buddhist point of view the usefulness of labor lies chiefly in its function of sustaining life, and life's value in turn derives from the possibility of attaining that wisdom which brings us into Truth. If labor is not needed to sustain us, then no real value is lost, for the aim of our life can now be pursued with more energy and more time than ever.

Boredom is the result of having nothing to do in which we are wholeheartedly invested, and destruction is the fruit of an ignorance about where our true good and deepest satisfaction lie—or of a sense of hopelessness about attaining them. Automation, therefore, offers us the possibility of an era when education shall aim not simply at making men capable of earning a living, but of valuing themselves for the wisdom they may attain. It could be an era, moreover, when all men shall have enough time for those disciplines of mind and body which are helpful in the pursuit of enlightenment. The "problem" of automation arises because our culture is misoriented and men are not trained from infancy to appreciate and explore the mystery that is life and life's meaning. The Japanese whose heart is warmed by the prospect of an evening of "moon-viewing" or the American who knows the rich harvest to be cultivated in his own introspective Walden cannot really look upon an increase of leisure with anything but delight, for it is in reflection, meditation, openness to nature, and relaxed wonder that life is lifted above the crass and trivial and made the vehicle for the attainment of ultimate meanings.

To put it briefly, I do not need economically productive work to achieve joy and fulfill the purpose of life. I can at least as readily be opened to the Truth by contemplating a cloud as by fulfilling my functions as a mechanic or a chairman of the board. Consequently the only genuine problem that leisure presents is the same problem that the need for work has always presented: How can people be guided to make it a means to the proper goal of mankind and not either meaningless passing of time or an end in itself?

Another problem that we discussed earlier is modern man's sense of uncertainty about himself and his value in a time when medical science is making him appear increasingly like a machine with interchangeable parts. How seriously can I take myself when I could conceivably be broken up surgically and reused to support the functions of a dozen other ailing bodies? Are we not confronted here with a new form of an old human enterprise that has always rather alarmed us—cannibalism?

One can imagine a Buddha's gentle smile if he were faced with this question. Why is anyone troubled about such a problem? Am I my liver? Am I my heart? Is there anything which *I* may be said to be? If there is, surely it is merely a consciousness, an awareness that contains memories and that has accepted certain values and ideas. Here, if anywhere, lies the seat of that "identity" which I mean when I use the word "myself." But what is this consciousness? Is it not merely a mode of the Absolute, is it not *Śūnyatā*? What is needful is that I shall step out of my concern for my person and particularity and know that *Śūnyatā* can, in its essence, experience no transplants! Nothing is destroyed; nothing is lost even in death, so how could it be lost in any sort of surgical manipulation? Or, rather, what may be lost and what, in any case, is always in danger, is that bedeviling, spurious little center of illusion which I call my ego. My fears arise because I want this puny straw in the wind to be immortal; I invest all my concern in this transient shadow. Let me lose my self-consciousness in an awakened consciousness of the Absolute Self and I have nothing to fear.

In fact, the enlightened man can gladly support every effort of the medical scientist to use whatever manipulations become possible for the support of human life, since to do so is to make possible the prolongation of a consciousness in which the rapture of enlightenment may occur.

Another problem for which *Mahāyāna*, with its emphasis on universalizing enlightenment, has an answer is that of each man's proper relationship to his society. In the West we have variously admired "rugged individualism," selfless dedication to the community, and an assortment of compromises between the two. For the Buddhist, the ideal pattern of social relationship should be reasonably clear, at least in broad outline.

Individualism can certainly not be a *Mahāyāna* ideal. Its stress on the value of the particular ego, its radical separation of man from man as though self-reliance were truly a possibility, is obviously not congenial to the *Śūnyatā* idea. The "self-made" man sufficient to himself is self-deceived because he does not understand that in the Truth there are no real distinctions. This is not quite the same as John Donne's "No man is an island," because Donne was doubtless thinking of the pattern of human relationships in a more or less linear fashion; our lives touch and interlock, so that what we do affects others and together we constitute a "whole" which, although more than the sum of its parts, does not cancel or eliminate the integrity of the parts. For the Buddhist, as we have seen, at the ultimate level of reality we do not have a "whole" which is a sort of aggregation of closely knit parts, but an indivisible Absolute free of distinctions. Since each man's temporal objective must be to assist the universalizing of enlightenment, and because no individual's attainment of wisdom is "full" until wisdom reigns everywhere (an inference from the *Śūnyatā* doctrine), individualism must be seen as a grossly unfortunate perpetuation of illusion. We cannot live to ourselves or for ourselves once we know that the very claim of the fundamental importance of individuality is a symptom of the disease that plunges the whole world into suffering and error.

On the other hand, most forms of social collectivism are also unacceptable to *Mahāyāna*. If individualism falsely isolates persons, nationalism and patriotism equally falsely isolate groups of persons. So does any form of racial or class prejudice. It must be reluctantly acknowledged that certain forms of Buddhism have expressed themselves in intensely nationalistic ways (Japan's *Nichiren* sect is the outstanding example), but these instances are aberrant and are usually rationalized into the likeness of orthodoxy by the participants. The decisive point to be made is this: To hate, despise, or exclude my neighbor is, in the last resort, to do no less to Śūnyatā.

Thus, the exclusiveness of most forms of collectivism ("my" group against "your" group) cannot be tolerated in the effort to extend to all beings the enlightenment that is Buddhism's goal.

But collectivism is often to be rejected for another reason as well. An attraction of mass-belonging is the sense of security it offers. As an individual I am small, vulnerable, and impotent. But if I belong, body and soul, to an aggregation sufficiently large, I feel secure in the collective power and I have a sense of identity derived from the identity of the group. This feeling of being "in" something of great or even ultimate value may insulate me from the Truth and may actually abort my quest for an authentic ultimate rootage in Śūnyatā. I am numbed and beguiled into complacency because if the question, "What am I?" ever struggles to consciousness, I can immediately bludgeon it with a phrase—"An American!" It seems likely that the more collectivist modern society becomes, the more strongly will therapeutic conditioning emerge as the mode of approved psychotherapy. To gain my reinforcement for socially acceptable responses is to become a veritable pillar of society —and to lose the impulse to ask more radical questions about my place in the scheme of things.

The alternative, then, to the forms of social relatedness we have rejected is a kind of extension of what is meant by the phrase, now familiar to us, "interpenetration of Absolutes."

If my enlightenment is not complete until all are enlightened; if I am the Absolute, but so are you; if our particularity is no illusion but real enough at its own level, I cannot ignore you and your need or what you have to offer me. Only by an inclusive mutuality in which simultaneously I acknowledge you as of unexcelled importance and know that the distinction of "you" and "I" is transcended at the deepest level of our being can I live the Truth.

This means that the proper mode of social relationships in this world is community in which we respect for what it is worth the temporal individuality of each man, but experience at the same time the unity of Being. We recognize that this unity is not simply the aggregation of separate persons, for that would be a collective merely; nor is it exclusive in a temporal sense—it is a unity undivided by the parade of generations as it is undivided by the separateness of persons.

But the unity we seek to experience is not static, so "Being" may not be a satisfactory word to name it unless we understand that this Being is also Becoming—dynamic, productive, yet essentially unfragmented. Community is the temporal, and therefore limited, expression of ultimate Truth if it knows no self-imposed boundaries, does not destroy the integrity of the individual, yet refuses to let him accept his isolated particularity as finally real. It is the symbol of the One without destroying the possibility for each of us to recognize himself not as an anonymous part of that One, but as the One itself. Such an understanding of oneself in relation to the absolute One is easy neither to express nor to experience, and the primary function of a community is to facilitate the experience by trying, in its structure and style of life, to approximate in temporal form the Truth which is Śūnyatā. The politics of community must be considered in a moment, but first we have sought merely to raise an image, imperfect no doubt, but perhaps suggestive.

In the last few pages we have been considering certain selected topics within the sphere of ethics, and before passing on to what may more properly be called politics a final note must be added about the place, in *Mahāyāna*, of rules or codes of conduct. *Mahāyāna* certainly accepts a considerable body of traditional Buddhist ethical teaching, but not without a difference that is consistent with its Absolutism and its basic ethical norm of *karunā* in the service of *prajñā*.

It is fair to say, I think, that the main objective of the entire body of ethical rules and regulations in non-*Mahāyāna* Buddhist systems has been the attainment of salvation or enlightenment for the individual who uses them to discipline himself. In the pursuit of this goal, morality (*sīla*) has always been regarded as indispensable and this has sometimes led to the observation (never wholly accurate and in *Mahāyāna* quite inaccurate) that Buddhism is more clearly an ethical system than a religious one.

A result of this is that Buddhist morality has sometimes tended toward a rigidity and inflexibility which puts principles ahead of persons and diverts the attention or concern of the practicer from others and their needs. Compassion, therefore, is often regarded as simply a stage of development which must be transcended before enlightenment can be fully experienced.

In *Mahāyāna* any tendency toward inflexibility or individualism is firmly corrected in accordance with the clear demands of a way of thinking which embraces as its most important premise the idea of Ultimate Reality as a dynamic Absolute. That "all are One," but a One which is manifest in each particular is an idea which, as we have seen, leads to the conclusion that enlightenment must be universal or it cannot be considered to be fulfilled in any particular being. *Mahāyāna* Absolutism, that is to say, leads directly to the conviction that each man's primary ethical obligation is to seek the universalizing of wisdom and this in turn leads to the idea that compassion for all men is an essential characteristic of the sage, never to be transcended so long as a wisp of illusion leaves a remnant of false individualism in existence.

Love or compassion, then, which seeks the enlightenment of all, must seek any other, secondary goal which will in any way facilitate the attainment of enlightenment. It cannot tolerate any condition that precludes the possibility of "awakening" occurring to someone. If deep poverty makes it necessary for a man to work so hard to support his family that he has no time to seek the cultivation of understanding, then that poverty cannot be a matter of indifference to the Buddhist. Similarly, physical suffering or danger, anxiety, fear, or any other possible human condition that becomes an obstacle to enlightenment must be attacked in love by the Buddhist who truly seeks to fulfill his obligation.

This means that conventional rules and codes are, in *Mahāyāna,* secondary to compassion, and although they ought not to be treated lightly if they carry the authority of the Buddha himself or of ancient tradition, neither ought they to be allowed to impede the unchallengeable priority of love and the extension of wisdom. Dogen, comparing a *śrāvaka* (a Buddhist but not a *Mahāyānist*) with a *bodhisattva,* says, "A *śrāvaka*'s abiding by the *sīla* might in some cases be replaced for the *bodhisattva* by the violation of the same *sīla*." [24] What he means is that the *śrāvaka,* aware that a regulation of his ethical code forbade his contact with women, would properly ignore the cry of a woman even if it might mean that she were in physical danger—perhaps drowning. A *Mahāyāna* sage, on the other hand, in a similar situation would set aside the rule against contact with women in order to help and thus obey the higher law of compassion. This does not mean that the saving of a woman's life could be an end in itself, but that her life is the "scene" in which she has an opportunity to meet the Truth, and the saving of it is therefore a means toward the end of the extension of understanding.

Further, as Dogen also makes clear in the *Shōbōgenzō,* an Absolutism of the *Mahāyāna* kind leads to the perception that ethical demand and ethically appropriate response are both as much *Śūnyatā* as any particular entity is, and therefore a measure of my personal progress toward enlightenment may be the degree to which my ethical decisions are not only proper but spontaneous. If I must think about rules and codes of conduct; if I must deliberate carefully and can produce suitable *Mahāyāna* behavior only with difficulty, it is clear that the wall of illusion and misdirected desire continues to separate "my" thought from the Truth. The enlightened man is he in whom the ethical demand and response have become his very subjectivity. In him, "being" and "doing" are one—the unborn and undying Truth. He is, therefore, beyond ethical struggle and may act without hesitation, naturally and spontaneously. There is no barrier of self-conscious reflection between the stimulus and his response. His acting *is* his being, and he needs no puzzled intermission between the impulse and the act.

Now we must move on to think about the relevance of *Mahāyāna* philosophy for a few of the contemporary problems of political life.

What could be considered the proper ideal of *Mahāyāna* politics? Such a question can be answered easily: it must be the same goal that unifies *Mahāyāna* ethics—the universalizing of *prajñā*. This means, speaking in the most general terms, that it is the function of a Buddhist political theory to propose a system of social organization which best facilitates the attainment and extension of the Buddhist experience of enlightenment, and every practical political decision and act must be measured by the yardstick of its positive or negative relation to this goal.

The participation of Buddhists in the political affairs of their nations is a long and complicated story, and one into which we cannot enter now. It is enough if we can show the shape of *Mahāyāna* politics and its relevance to major issues confronting mankind today.

In Buddhaghosa's very important fifth-century work, the *Visuddhimagga*, we find outlined a theory of the state which excellently illustrates what I believe to be the appropriate tenor of Buddhist political theory. Here is a social compact concept of society propounded in conjunction with a notion of kingship by a sort of contract. Society is justified as a phenomenon by its organized facilitating of the quest for *Nirvāna*. It is easier, in a properly constituted state, for individuals to seek their spiritual fulfillment than it would be if they remained isolated, since by a wise division of labor each man can be given some free time and opportunity to pursue the disciplines of mind and body which prepare the way for *satori*.

But it is not true that *any* society is better than none, or that any government is good. On the contrary, one can imagine a society in which the manipulation of popular opinion produced a climate most uncongenial to Buddhism or in which the many were so exploited by the few that only the latter had time to cultivate anything but rice. We need a social structure, then, and a government bent upon the enlarging of every man's opportunity for advancement toward Truth.

An implication of the *Visuddhimagga* is that the ideal king would be a *bodhisattva,* a man of enormous enlightenment himself who is dedicated to the spreading of that happy state. He is expected to exercise his authority in the interests of the religious quest, striving to obtain the well-being and security of his subjects, who, finding themselves surrounded by suitable economic, social, and political conditions, are encouraged by his example to live the kind of life that is everyone's road to salvation. Thus, it is not hard to understand why throughout Southeast Asia the *sangha,* or order of monks, has been historically very closely associated with the throne, the king often being a protector of the prerogatives of the order, and the monks serving as advisers to the king.

This is clear enough, and it is obvious that kingship can be replaced by some other mode of government provided the same objective is retained: a parliament composed of two or more parties could be quite satisfactory if the basic principle on which it operated was government of the people by the (at least partially) enlightened, for the promoting of enlightenment. Practically, of course, a Buddhist today must reconcile himself at best to participating in a government whose responsibilities he shares with men who belong to different religious traditions or none at all, and in this case the Buddhist politician ought to strive to achieve at least that compromise for his people which most closely approximates the ideal.

It is important to notice that it is the goal of universalizing *prajñā* which justifies a system of government and a socioeconomic structure. An oligarchy or even a dictatorship that served this purpose well should be preferred to participatory democracy which obscured it. Indeed, although some version of democratic government may serve the *Mahāyāna* purpose well, the fact that most people live in a high degree of illusion and ignorance and therefore do not customarily choose wisely, leads to the conclusion that the most effective government would be government by an elite of enlightened persons. Such a government might be autocratic, but it would do its work in the true interests of the people and so serve them better than they could serve themselves.

But what kind of social and economic theory best permits the fulfillment of Buddhist social goals? Clearly, not one that is the vehicle of an *oppressive* authoritarianism. One cannot legislate *satori,* and Buddhists are not saved by fiat. The kind of society suggested in *Brave New World* or *A Clockwork Orange,* or even Skinner's disarmingly naïve *Walden Two* would not be agreeable to Buddhists because conditioned responses, however socially harmonious, are the opposite of enlightened understanding, which must come from within the individual where the Truth has always lain, however concealed it has been by the dense fog of misunderstanding. Perhaps the best paradigm of Buddhist government is the Zen master, or the "Good Friend" of the Pure Land Sects. That is, the government would be one that encouraged in every way the individual's personal pursuit of Truth and, if it ever acted harshly, did so not to determine the behavior of its subjects but (paradoxically) to force them to discover their freedom and in freedom to seek the Truth which lies within. Life, Liberty, and the Pursuit of Wisdom would be the formula—a better one, it seems to me, than its counterpart in the United States, since happiness is not an end to be pursued, but is discovered as the by-product of the attainment of something else—perhaps wisdom.

We must still ask, however, what kind of structure the ideal Buddhist society might assume in the modern world. Of the options we can most readily think about, would it resemble free-enterprise capitalism? Surely not, because the profit motive upon which such a system heavily rests is contrary to the

Buddhist ideal of overcoming the particular ego and its material advantage. Would it, then, be socialist? I believe so, but there are varieties of socialism and not all are equally congenial to Buddhist ideals. To understand this, let us consider some typical Buddhist reactions to Marxism.

In a day when Christian theologians are finding their dialogue with Marxist philosophers growing richer and more exciting, it should not surprise us to discover that Buddhists are also busy thinking and talking about Communism in various forms. The issue of theism *versus* atheism, diminishing in importance for many Marxists anyway, has never been a great problem in discussions with Buddhists, since Buddhism is indifferent to the idea of deity and has shown a remarkable ability to adapt itself to the wishes of local populations on the subject.

Moreover, there are a few significant Buddhist ideas that seem to lend themselves quite readily to a Marxist interpretation. Poverty and wealth are alike impediments to the quest for *Nirvāna*, the former because it may limit a man's freedom to devote time to religious ends, and the latter because it may make a man satisfied with this temporary and illusion-ridden existence. Consequently, a social system that abolished private property and attempted to regulate the production, distribution, and exchange of goods would seem to be a reasonable way of pursuing Buddhist goals. With the nationalization of the means of production and dispersal of material objects one could, at one fell swoop, deliver the poor from the poverty which cripples their hope of self-improvement, and the rich from the seductive bonds of their spiritually worthless affluence.

Removing the lure of private property rights would also, it must be said, seem to many Buddhists to prepare the way for peace in the world. In presenting a law to nationalize land, U Nu said to his Burmese parliament in October, 1948:

> World history is on the whole a record of continual warfare between a group of men and the masses . . .

because they do not get the right views regarding what is known as property. . . . Property is not meant to be saved, or for gain. It is to be used by men to meet their needs in their journey towards Nirvana.[25]

Nirvāna itself, or the goal of universal enlightenment, leads to a concern for economics and may be held to imply the nationalization of property, if that seems to be the most efficient way of removing the inequities which inhibit a general public movement toward Truth. It is precisely in this area of thought that Marxism appeals most strongly to Buddhists, and at times its appeal is very great indeed. A Burmese minister of war said in 1951:

> Actually, Marxist theory is not antagonistic to Buddhist philosophy. . . . Marxist theory refers to worldly affairs and seeks to satisfy material needs. Buddhist philosophy, however, deals with spiritual things, with the aim of liberation from this world.[26]

But there are Buddhist criticisms to be made of Marxism. Many Buddhists express doubt about the economic determinism in Marxist theory and insist that this is to see things much too superficially. It is not economics that determines man's situation; on the contrary, economics merely provides one way of describing that situation. It is *karma*, the inexorable and impersonal law of cause and effect, working its way relentlessly through history that firmly determines the circumstances of our lives, and although it is important to deal with economic injustice, we should not attribute to our doing so more significance than it really bears. To assume that any kind of merely economic reform can be more than a useful step toward the solution of human problems is to be credulous indeed, and to fail to understand the essential relatedness of all life as the *Śūnyatā* doctrine understands it is to fall easy victim to such superficiality.

Again, Communist *preoccupation* with materialistic values is not to be endorsed by a Buddhist who sees the material merely as a means to a spiritual end. To place too much emphasis on the material is, even in the absence of private property, to be drawn into a pluralistic and crassly empirical philosophy which may well deepen the darkness of our minds and carry us farther from enlightenment. The corrosive power of our spurious egotism is such that many a Buddhist would see a grave danger in any form of materialism, for men will find ways to defeat the leveling intention of the nationalization of property unless the real human problem, egocentricity, is attacked as Buddhism attacks it.

Many Buddhists are frankly alarmed at the Communist penchant for revolution, since this makes a *principle* of the violation of the doctrine of nonviolence (*ahimsā*) so dear to Buddhism, and even if it is conceded that there may be situations when revolution is the last remaining means to an end which Buddhists endorse, it must never be regarded as a norm or as a form of behavior easily resorted to.

Finally, the elevation of the state in Marxism is usually unacceptable to *Mahāyānists*, since the state should exist to further the opportunities of its people to strive for *Nirvāna*. It cannot be an end in itself or the ultimate authority for life.

But socialism is not necessarily tied to the aspects of Marxism to which Buddhists object, and when a man views the social and economic conditions of much of the world, and allows his ideal of love in the service of wisdom to operate as a critical principle, some form of socialism certainly seems to offer the best hope for a reasonable and constructive community. A system in which luxury is avoided and abject poverty is overcome will clearly do most good for most people.

The Buddhist, then, finds within his religious tradition the grounds for a political opinion and political action which, whether one values them or not, must be conceded to be relevant. His is *not* a religion of political docility or one that lacks the ground for critical appraisal of the *status quo*.

In the foreseeable future, however, it is unlikely that there will be a state, even in Buddhist lands, where public opinion is

undivided on important matters. What would Buddhist politicians do, if consistent with basic *Mahāyāna* ideas, with the
problem of dissent? Would this be permissible, and under what
conditions would it be allowed?

We are not concerned here with a history of Buddhism, so
will not attempt to trace the various ways in which Buddhist
authorities have regarded the dissenter. It seems to me to be
possible to specify some facets of a consistent *Mahāyāna* theory
with regard to dissent, and this is all that we are at present
obliged to do.

Certain principles must come to the fore when a *Mahāyānist*
government faces the fact of open disagreement among its
people. First, it governs in the interests of the people and must
therefore seek above all to establish the conditions in which
authentic wisdom is discoverable by all. It cannot, therefore,
crush every spark of free expression, for to do so would be to
preclude the liberty of spirit in which Buddhist inquiry can
best flourish. On the other hand, if a *Mahāyāna* government is
government by men of enlightenment—or at least a relative
degree of enlightenment—must not dissent from its way be
supposed to arise chiefly from men in a state of error? Must it
not, then, be unenlightened dissent? And if so, can one reasonably allow it to threaten the government's program which
aims at the universalizing of the perception of Truth?

A problem that will, presumably, always confuse the issue
is the selection of men of true wisdom to form a government.
One can hardly entertain the illusion that politicians report
accurately their own character, and in the most dedicatedly
Buddhist country it is easy to imagine errors of judgment on
the part of electors or appointers. There is always the possibility, therefore, that dissent may express a greater measure of
Buddhist insight than the policies of the government, and in
a land which cherished Buddhist ideals it would consequently
be necessary to protect the right of dissent—or at least to
protect dissent's right to prove itself correct if it can.

Yet the fact remains that a government which believed that

it genuinely served the people by its faithfulness to Buddhist principles would inevitably be reluctant to allow dissent to operate destructively or to precipitate revolution. There are, of course, many decisions that a government must make which would have little to do with establishing the optimal conditions for a people's search for *prajñā*, and in regard to these a great deal of liberty for dissent may be permitted. But if I, as a Buddhist statesman, believed that my policies were establishing conditions in which that which is most important in human life can be accomplished by the people I serve, I would feel that dissent aimed at those policies was an attack upon the well-being of my people. It must therefore be allowed only a restricted area of movement. Sadly enough, this was the logic of the European Inquisitor, and even if a modern Buddhist wisely avoided burning his heretics, there are great dangers requiring the utmost delicacy of handling. Yet it is hard to see how the Buddhist could justify permitting the heretic enough freedom of expression to endanger the eternal values sought for all men by the government.

In short, a Buddhist, whether in the government or the official or unofficial opposition, must be dedicated to the universalizing of enlightenment. As an opponent of the Establishment, he may be led by this to some kind of revolution (although violence must never be more than a desperate last resort at best). As the established authority, on the other hand, the Buddhist must surely be led by his ideal to a deep concern for the revolutionary, but an unwillingness to permit revolution to gather momentum.

The ultimate goal of Buddhism is of unconditional value. *Nirvāna* is the *only* proper destination for man. Therefore, so long as love is not needlessly sacrificed, almost any means (*upāya*) to the end of universal enlightenment should be accepted. If one has an absolute value, as the *Mahāyānist* certainly has, any other value is thereby relativized, and this would include freedom for dissent. It must be understood, however, that we are not speaking here about the individual's right to choose for himself other values and goals than Buddhist ones. We are talking only about more or less organized, outspoken, and enacted deviation that threatens to obstruct the establishment of Buddhist values as a social norm. And we are not saying that any Buddhist government or politician will inevitably favor the suppression of any dissent that reaches dangerous proportions. We have merely shown a line of argument by which such suppression may be justified.

I am sure that most ardent Buddhists would hope that the social and economic equity they would establish, the justice for all regardless of "rank" or reputation, and the sensitivity to remediable suffering which would be their concern, would make their government acceptable to Buddhists and non-Buddhists alike, and would restrict serious dissent to a few ego-centered malcontents incapable of perceiving their own best interests. To love such people is to seek their good, even if their true good is precisely what they are presently resisting. No one gives a baby a bottle of poison, even if it is what he wants; anyone will give him milk instead. This is not to deny him any important "right," but merely to recognize that he is not yet capable of knowing what is in his own interest.

Before we conclude this chapter something must be said about a *Mahāyāna* view of man's place in and responsibility for nature, and about the uses and abuses of technology. On both of these subjects many books could be written (and therefore doubtless will be), but we will be satisfied now to indicate briefly a few central ideas.

Pre-Darwinian Western opinion tended to see man as essentially discontinuous with nature in important respects. That is to say, he was a part of the natural order, of course, but a part of it so different from any other that the differences were more important than the similarities. Pre-Copernican thought even tended to place man on a pinnacle and to derive the meaning and value of the entire universe from him. His world lay in the center of the cosmos, and in that world man was the creature for whom all the rest had been made.

Now that we know that our planet is one of an unimaginable number, is not the center even of our own planetary system, and very well may not be the only one bearing intelligent life, many people are uncertain about their status in the natural order.

Again, science and technology have made strides in the West that make the puny efforts of Easterners astonishing only for their insignificance. On the one hand, Western science has dispelled our illusion about man's radical superiority in essence, and on the other it has truly placed us at the pinnacle of the natural order, giving us power to manipulate the resources of our planet for our comfort and advantage in ways beyond the dreaming even of Jules Verne. And there is no doubt that the Orient waits like a gasping and emaciated man for the gift of our technical excellence. His exhausted fields need Western skills and equipment; his starved economy needs an infusion of the steel blood of industry.

There is, however, a tarantula hidden in the ripe fruit of Western science and technology, and we have been bitten and are not sure yet whether or how soon the venom will prove fatal. We have learned how to build the most affluent civilization the world has seen (although, be it confessed, outrageously uneven in the distribution of its affluence), but almost without our noticing, an ogre has been hatched by our efforts. We face the dissipation of our natural resources, the ineradicable pollution of rivers and atmosphere, and the loss of natural beauty to an extent that may make human survival, even if possible, not so very attractive. Not that this has happened suddenly, but even now we are so slow to recognize the disease in our midst that one fears it may be irreversible before enough people see it to bring about the kind of reform that is needed. We are rather like the man who lost his hair gradually over many years until only one hair was left. This he brushed and oiled assiduously every morning and every night, until one day he awoke to find it lying on his pillow. Staring at it with unbelieving horror, he gasped, "My God! I'm bald."

What, then, has Buddhism to say to this situation? What is

man's place in nature, and what values should govern his use of technology?

Believers in *Śūnyatā* can never think themselves very separate from the rest of nature. In the Void all distinctions are overcome and a man is therefore not properly to be seen as against nature or above it, but with it and in it. What happens to nature happens to us and the pollution of a river is the defilement of ourselves.

But man, as the most developed intelligence among sentient beings, has, for that reason, unique responsibilities. In him nature rises to responsibility, for in him is the birth of ethics, morality, and the possibility of enlightenment. A lion kills a lamb, and one may pity the lamb but one can hardly condemn the lion. It is men who must make a decision about whether or not they will kill to eat, for they alone among creatures can think about what it means to kill.

There have been many Buddhists who chose not to eat meat, and the Buddha himself seems to have taught his disciples that they might eat it only if they did not know that the beast had been killed for their express benefit. In a day when we are beginning to take seriously the possibility that plants and vegetables may also be sensitive, in some sense, to pain, a great many Buddhists recognize that a prohibition against meat-eating hardly solves the problem of causing suffering. They eat what they will, but recognize that the very impossibility of sustaining physical life without inflicting suffering is a continuous and terrible indication that such life is not the jewel we are prone to think it, but is inextricably involved in anguish. To exist is not only inevitably to suffer, but to inflict suffering.

He who knows all this is bound, however, to take his treatment of nature seriously. He cannot be flippant even about a fly, and he sees that the ethical ideal of nonviolence is truly an ideal and as such includes all beings in its range of compassion. A modern Buddhist in an industrialized society may smile a little at his fellows of other times and places who strained their drinking water lest they inadvertently swallow a minuscule piece of life, and laboriously brushed the path before them lest they tread on something too small to be seen, but he does not laugh at their concern; he shares it. He knows that every act by which a man wantonly destroys or corrupts a fragment of the universe is an act which impoverishes him, for he is that which he has assailed.

Now, all of this means that our sense of human value, dealt severe blows by Copernicus, Darwin, and many others, is, in one way, given its final push into the grave, while in another way it is renewed inviolably. As this particular entity, as this scrap of the universe, I who bear this name and live at that address am unimportant indeed, being neither above nature nor of any great intrinsic value as an individual. But when, forsaking my ego, I plunge into that depth of awareness in which "I" dissolve and become Truth, Suchness, *Śūnyatā*, I am discovered as that which does not care about its value because its value is infinite and invulnerable. Returning to a consciousness of my particularity, I rejoice in what I have discovered about my deeper Self, and know that my rejoicing is not for myself alone but for all that I encounter. I would now no more wish to pollute a stream than swallow dirt, and if I am involved in industry, it is with a new concern for the environment with which I sense an indissoluble bond.

Here, then, is the root of a *Mahāyāna* view of nature and technology. To borrow Western terms, we may say that since nothing is less sacred than anything else, nothing may be wantonly exploited or debased by anything else, and especially not by man, whose special qualities of awareness make him the threshold of universal awakening. But if, as some analysts now cheerlessly affirm, the rape of this planet has already proceeded so far that its demise and ours is irreversible, even this is not a matter to desolate the Buddhist. He has never insisted that earth was the only scene in which the drama of Being was enacted or that it is indispensable to the Truth. A lump of matter swirling in space and some animate species on it are endangered by the consequences of a blinding ignorance and illusion. So be it. *Śūnyatā* is not about to become extinct!

Nevertheless, while our planet and our human lives persist,

the Buddhist cheerfully assumes responsibility for proclaiming and encouraging the universalizing of *prajñā,* and he addresses every practical problem and dilemma with a unifying principle: love in the service of enlightenment. There can be no problem which does not yield to this key in some fashion. Are we alarmed at the prospect of overpopulation? Let us recognize that sexual satisfaction is not the most rewarding of human experiences, and that there is no cosmic demand for the continual production of children, but that every Buddhist, man or woman, must seek first the fulfillment of wisdom and that this demands the restraint of physical appetite in the interests of spiritual satisfaction. In short, if having children is seen as impeding the quest for total enlightenment in any way (for instance, by so reducing the standards of living among men that they are left with no energy or resources for anything but mere survival), then the Buddhist knows what he must do. He must support with all his energy every program to reduce population expansion, but this is not merely in the interests of human comfort and contentment: it is in the interest of his constant objective—the eventual dispelling of the last vestiges of illusion.

In very summary fashion we have seen in this chapter that *Mahāyāna* does indeed address itself to contemporary problems of the most practical kind. We have not dealt specifically with every issue raised in Part One, nor have we followed the labyrinthine implications of the problems we did deal with to the last minute point of their extension. Enough has been said, however, to indicate the direction of the kind of answers that I would find appropriate to this day. We shall reserve a final chapter in this section for a mercifully brief conclusion.

V

Destiny and Decision

Ah, for the heart whose winter knew no doubt!
—*Mokuin*

Earlier in this inquiry we asked some questions which, it was hoped, our discussion would help to answer: What is man? What is his appropriate mode of being in the world? What is his destiny or ultimate possibility? In short, what dream may a man dream today? In the last few chapters we have seen an outline of one possible answer, drawn from the vast, complex, and ancient Buddhist tradition, and it remains for us now only to summarize a few of its most prominent features and to say a final word about human destiny.

What is man? At the level of everyday experience man is a being whose very existence entails suffering for himself and others. Most seriously, that existence and its particularity entrap him into a false view of reality, including his own reality, so that he attributes value where there is none and permanence to the dissolving mists of mundane forms. He fights and kills for possession of trivia. He persecutes in defense of ideas and values that have no substance. He tortures himself with a thousand nameless fears (and as many that have names!) because he has not mastered the first lesson in the curriculum of Reality—that Truth and Value are hidden behind the errors and disvalues which he adores.

What is man? At the heart of Truth one can find no words to answer this question, for the Truth is elusive if we chase it with a net of logic, but docile if we seek it in immediate experience, in that intuitive openness which the mental and physical disciplines of Buddhism aim to cultivate. But if words cannot trap the Truth, there are words which, better than others, may point roughly in its direction.

A man is the Void; he is Suchness; he is the Buddha-Mind; he is the Unborn. Beyond particularity (but within it too) he is the Absolute without distinctions. As we have generally chosen to say in this book, he is *Śūnyatā*. This means that in himself each man is victim and victor, oppressed and oppressor, and in true understanding or wisdom he becomes free of the futility of both. He may enjoy the light, the warmth, the cooling breeze, the autumn leaf, because he is these things in a splendid continuity which overcomes all barriers, and he may fear no death because the Reality he is contains the death of all particulars but never dies.

Our destiny, therefore, is what the *Mahāyāna* Buddhist means when he speaks the word "*Nirvāna*." This is not a place (as heaven or paradise are, for the wise Westerner, not places) but a condition, a state of being, a tranquil splendor. *Nirvāna* is the state of having died to the vulnerable particular self and its clamorous demands and of having found oneself to be the Universal Self, no less. *Nirvāna* is the extinction of the flickering candle of particularity in the golden glow of unquenchable Being. *Nirvāna* is the state in which one does not simply *know* the Truth, but knows oneself to *be* the Truth.

The *Mahāyāna* mode of being in the world, therefore, is to be the Truth even in the midst of apparent chaos; and this means to personify compassion in the service of the universalizing of understanding.

Mahāyāna does not teach that an enlightened man must fly from the world or forsake it, for *Nirvāna* is not some "other place" to which he goes. It *is* the world. As a popular Buddhist saying has it, *Nirvāna* is *Samsāra*. This is true because, when we learn to view things from the perspective of the ultimate and true nature of Reality, there is nothing (no self-existent, independent thing) entering or leaving existence. To see the world, knowing what one truly is, is to see the world as *Nirvāna* or *Śūnyatā* (which, of course, are really synonyms); to see the same world *without* knowing what one truly is, is to see a confusion of apparently real, separate, and multiple things and to find oneself threatened and insecure.

Men ordinarily try to achieve completeness by adding to their store more and more possessions. This is to try to protect the frail particular ego by erecting around it a wall of things, but since none of these things has the power to endure forever, we remain weak and unprotected. The true road to completeness consists of losing the ego, which is the self-conscious focus of our individuality, and finding ourselves as the infinite Self beyond distinctions and the possibility of corruption. But this self-abandonment and Self-discovery are not reserved for some ethereal plane removed from daily life. On the contrary, they are to experienced in the context of daily life, and when they are, the meaning and the value of that life are magnificently transformed. *Nirvāna* is *Samsāra*. And since *Samsāra* means involvement in the life of the world, its politics, its industry, its wealth and poverty and everything else, *Nirvāna* is a way of experiencing and living within all that constitutes the troubled spectrum of our days.

So *Mahāyāna* offers a word for men today. It offers a way of facing the difficulties of this time, and answers to the insistent questions of our life. But is it the *correct* word? As the redoubtable Father Brown remarks in one of Chesterton's stories: "Ten false philosophies will fit the universe; ten false theories will fit Glengyle Castle. But we want the real explanation of the castle and the universe." [27] Is *Mahāyāna's* the *real* explanation? How can one know?

The final evidence for *Mahāyāna* must lie in experience. If, after studying *Mahāyāna* ideas and following *Mahāyāna* disciplines you enjoy the experience which is variously called *satori,* enlightenment, awakening, or *samādhi*—if, that is, you actually experience the subjugation of the particular ego and the birth of awareness of Ultimacy, you may then feel that the case is proven. To have this experience is certainly to see the world thereafter through different eyes. It is to become a new man. It is to know, beyond a shadow of doubt, that *Mahāyāna* penetrates all the problems of the universe with light. To have such an experience is to *become Mahāyāna* Truth, and the *Mahāyānist* rightly invites you to follow him to that discovery, knowing that if you do, you will find it more persuasive than an infinity of argument.

But *satori* is a subjective experience. It may be an experience of Truth, but can this be proved? Here lies a difficulty for men educated in the Western tradition. They know that nothing is more elusive than subjective reliability. Speaking about mystical experience in general, William James said:

> (1) Mystical states, when well developed, usually are, and have the right to be, absolutely authoritative over the individuals to whom they come.

> (2) No authority emanates from them which should make it a duty for those who stand outside of them to accept their revelations uncritically.[28]

Still, the Buddhist says: The proof of my way lies in experience, not speculation. The experience is to be had by ancient and tested disciplines, not by convenient shortcuts such as hallucinogenic drugs or the lazy simplifications of jet-set gurus, and you will never know the truth or otherwise of *Mahāyāna* until you make the journey it prescribes. Here hangs the issue, and here we must leave it, for neither this book nor any other can carry you into the Buddhist experience itself.

Part Three
CHRISTIANITY

VI
The Lost

"You can't get there from here."

A man may not know how lost he is until he has been found. It is possible to wander in a forest, seeming to recognize a hundred landmarks and to find at last that all these recognitions were deceptive, the fruit of imagination and desire. Nothing one experiences, no degree of confidence, no powerful conviction, no blazing sense of Truth or illumination, is ever beyond question.

None of us, therefore, can escape the need for a frequent sifting of our beliefs. Neither the philosopher whose clearly reasoned argument may be no more than a rationalization to justify what he wants to believe, nor the scientist who unconsciously selects and edits the very data he then examines and interprets with far less objectivity than he imagines, nor the mystic whose "awakening" to Truth may be the subtlest illusion of all, nor that legendary animal the "Common Man" in whom nothing is less common than common sense. And here is a convenient place to begin our discussion of Christianity.

The Christian concedes that his own beliefs are as much in need of critical attention as any, for he knows that however certain a man may feel about his convictions and the experiences upon which these rest, absolute certainty eludes us forever in this life, and he who does not understand this is the most endangered of us all. Yet the Christian nourishes within himself an experience and critically cultivates some convictions which seem to him to open wide vistas of understanding and even to explain the persistent human tendency to make mistakes about the goals and meanings of life.

Men are lost, and do not know they are lost. We follow false trails in search of meaning and spend our lives in futile effort because we are estranged from that to which we belong and in which our destiny and meaning lie. We are proud with a pride which makes us literally unable to understand the truth and highly susceptible to the deepest convictions about certain kinds of falsehood. But this pride may not wear the honest face of arrogance. It may disguise itself as humility and assure us that we have utterly eliminated our ego when we have, in fact, merely so enlarged it that it has absorbed the universe and can consequently no longer be identified as what it is. To see how hopeless man's state of lostness is, let us consider a Christian appraisal of that most convincing and religious of all human experiences, the mystical.

The mystical experience has been variously defined, but we shall be content to say that it is the sense of having broken through the ordinary limits of perception to grasp a wholly new and utterly convincing view of life, the universe, and everything. It entails a feeling of being united with (or of having discovered oneself to be) that indestructible and essentially indivisible Ultimate Reality which is the only final Truth.

Such an experience, in its fullness, comes to only a few persons, but it is composed of certain elements that are more common. First, it includes as a precondition a sensitivity to mystery. "Mystery" here does not mean ignorance. ("Mystery stories" should really be called "ignorance stories" because their problem is a lack of information, and as soon as we learn how, when, where, and why the butler "done it" there is no "mystery" left.)

Mystery is a quality in things that is not dissolved by any amount of information. If one knew all there was to know about a stone, it would still be possible to be lost in wonder at the very presence, the sheer facticity of the thing. Such wonder is common to a child, but we have never found the trick of keeping it alive, and sheer familiarity with the world dries it up in all but the poet and, occasionally, other sensitive spirits among us. He who has never been strangely thrilled by something he perfectly understood will not know what I am trying to say, and he who has will need no more than what I have said, so we shall pass on to the second element in mystical awareness.

Next we must include the intuitive, immediate, and total apprehension of something. Who of us has not had a teacher carefully explain the steps in the solving of some mathematical problem, so that after a time we could take a similar problem and by imitation laboriously work it out step by step? Finally, we remember the steps and no longer have to consult the paradigm. But still it is labored; still it is a mechanical, step-by-step process. At last, one day, in a flash of comprehension we "see" the process as a whole, we understand, as it were, the meaning of it. We see it now not as a series of calculations but as a total thing. We feel as if a light has dawned. We no longer worry about forgetting one of the steps, for there is nothing mechanical or piecemeal about our working now. This is one variant of the experience of intuitive, immediate apprehension, and it too is an element in the mystic's sudden enlightenment, his immediate grasp of life.

Third, there is the loss of awareness of self, of effort, or of the object of our effort in a moment of total absorption. No one who can read and has imagination is wholly unfamiliar with this. Late at night, having graded the last intolerable student essay for the day and having dutifully read enough of the professional rubbish my vocation imposes upon me, I settle in a comfortable chair and pick up the latest product of the genius of Ngaio Marsh or John Creasey. The persons in the story quickly become "real" for me, their situation desperate and intriguing. Finally comes a moment when I am quite unaware of myself, the book, and the act of reading, for all have become one. Now, if this experience occurs not simply with a story, but with the cosmos; if I lose self-consciousness and consequently awareness of the otherness of the universe and of my act of perceiving it, so that the universe, myself, and my relations with it become a "one" in which I experience no distinctions, I have attained another element in the mystic's experience of reality. I am not, of course, talking about the situation in which, perhaps through fatigue, one becomes simply unaware; I am talking about a situation in which distinctions are transcended while awareness remains intense.

Finally, and largely as an aspect in or facilitator of this last element, there is what Freud called the "oceanic feeling" which may be, as he suggested, a heritage of our prenatal experience and which is more easily recaptured by some people than by others. Before a child suffers that first separation which is his birth he can hardly be aware of distinctions. If he has any sort of awareness at all, it must be without definition, a simple awareness of being—truly an "oceanic" kind of feeling. At any rate, some persons seem to be haunted throughout their lives by a longing for the lost paradise of nondistinction, for the condition which existed before they learned to say "I" and "mine," and to know the vulnerability which we experience as individuals who can be isolated, can suffer loss and die. And this longing may sometimes be rewarded by the momentary recovery of the sense of being not this lonely, particular self, but the All, the One which is everything without ceasing to be One.

These, then, are at least some elements in the mystical, and there are disciplines of mind and body which, if we pursue them diligently, will help us to attain their fusion in one momentous, totally absorbing experience. There are also drugs which, it would seem, can do as much for us, although this remains open to question. *From a Christian point of view, however, such an experience is still the experience of lost men and may as easily be a deepening of their lostness as a part of their being found.* For it is the experiencing man himself in all his capacities who is estranged from his true belonging and he can only "see" what a lost man can see until something from that to which he belongs comes to him.

In short, man's mystical capacity is like his ordinary power of vision. It really functions and it is valuable, but it can be mistaken and it can be directed to the wrong object. If it is drawn to that which has a right to claim us, the richest kind of human experience ensues, but it can be so drawn only when that to which we belong signals and attracts our attention. Otherwise, we will bend our mystical vision in an inappropriate direction. Perhaps we shall turn it in upon ourselves, in which case we experience the same absorption, elation, tranquillity, and assurance that mysticism always brings but our self shall have become our god. Or we may direct it to the cosmos, in which case we are plunged into a sense of oneness with the universe—with Being—which is endlessly satisfying and dissipates our fears and our loneliness, however spuriously. Indeed, we might go farther and say that when the mystical capacity is directed inward so that the self is elevated to become the Absolute Self (although this is not usually recognized as what is occurring) we have performed spiritual masturbation. When the mystical vision is directed to an inappropriate object such as the cosmos, we have spiritual adultery.

For a Christian, then, the mystic's experience is cognitively inconclusive of any truth but one: that men may be or become sensitive to mystery.

This possible sensitivity is, however, an important human datum. No one who fails to take it seriously can really understand the human adventure on this planet, or even some parts of the purely intellectual segment of that adventure. The history of philosophy, for example, is littered with the wreckage of attempts to construct an infallible "proof" of the existence of God, but what was really important about these pseudo proofs was not their logic or their empirical validity, but the fact that they touched and gave a sort of voice to something profoundly moving in the experience of men—a sense of wonder. No one can demonstrate that this world needs an Unmoved Mover or a First Cause; but when some of us ask the question why there is anything at all, we know that all rational answers are amusing, and the absence of an answer unsatisfying. The question goes beyond the reach of rationality, and when we allow ourselves simply to be open to it, to try to experience the sheer fact of there being something, we become aware that we are encountering an infinite and transcendent mystery. Yet, it must be repeated, in his ordinary mystical response man misnames that mystery unless it names itself and speaks a word about itself to us in some way that moves beyond the murky depths of our subjectivity and impinges on the objective world itself. Unless, in short, that which we may encounter in our own depths as an Ultimate Reality transcends those depths to become concretely historical we have reason to suspect that we are focused upon an invention of our own imagination rather than that in which object and subject alike are maintained.

Here, then, is the ground on which Christianity rises. Man's lostness entails ignorance and pride, and produces an abundant harvest of sloth, indifference, self-centeredness, cruelty, suspicion—and religion! The best that we could do to mitigate the sufferings of life would be to control or eliminate desire, to cultivate compassion and restraint. But all this changes, and new possibilities and hopes arise if, incredibly, the mystery we have dimly seen in the universe does indeed present itself to us in an intelligible way and, even without resolving all our questions, offers at least a pinpoint of light which moves ahead of us to show us the direction of our destiny.

It is precisely the "news" that this has happened that is the "gospel" of Christianity.

VII

The Finding

What bloody man is that?
—*Shakespeare,*
Macbeth, *Act I, Scene ii*

Authentic Christianity is the repudiation of all religion.

Having enjoyed writing that sentence I must now, of course, admit that it is true only for certain understandings of the word "religion," but these include one which I would judge to be the most common of all. Religion is often, and quite legitimately, regarded as man's way of seeking to discover and relate to the final, most "real" Reality, whether this is called the Absolute, Being, God, Brahman, or anything else. In this sense there are several forms which religion takes, and these are not mutually exclusive, so that any particular person's religious life may give evidence of all of them. They are: (1) the rational; (2) the mystical; (3) the practical.

The rational seeking of the Ultimate Reality tends to be a fairly dispassionate enterprise ranging from responsible philosophy at one end of its spectrum to bizarrely elaborate constructions of superstition and speculation at the other. The mystical tends to be a non- or even anti-intellectual quest for an immediate grasping of and union with the Ultimate, and the practical consists of a range of activities that are thought to bring one into satisfactory relation with whatever deserves to be called "God." These activities include rituals, good deeds, and even magic. Common to all these forms of religion is the spirit of quest: they are means for reaching that ultimacy in which Truth, Beauty, Life, and all values find their source and fullness.

Christianity, on the other hand, began as the astonished recognition that Ultimacy had always been disclosing itself in some sense, but had finally done so in a unique and definitive way. To many men of intellectual or spiritual pride, this was an intolerably annoying claim because it implied that all their efforts—their religions—were futile and misdirected, but to the unpretentious who responded it was extraordinarily liberating and exhilarating. Christianity was established, not as one more way to find God, but as the joyful response of men who knew that they had been found.

Henceforth, for the Christians, rituals and good deeds might be important but they could never be essential, and magic must be excluded altogether because the Ultimate who has disclosed and given himself is seen to be one who cannot be bought, bribed, bullied, or in any way manipulated. The significance of the abused doctrine of the virgin birth of Christ is the perception that God's actions are never at man's mandate. There might be mountains of speculation—philosophy and theology enough to make the cosmos groan—but even it and its correctness or incorrectness is not to be decisive for man's attainment of the Truth which is God. Even mystical experience, although thrilling and valuable, is not what finally matters. One thing alone is needed now: to recognize the self-disclosure of God in the remarkable phenomenon named Jesus and now given the title "Christ," and to respond with faith and gratitude. To be united with the Christ through one's trust in him, through one's simple acceptance of him as God's tangible offer of peace and reconciliation—this is the beginning of the life whose end is fulfillment. Jesus himself is reported to have said, "I have come that men may have life, and may have it in all its fullness." (John 10:10‡.) To accept this as true is, so the Christian declares, to accept God's acceptance of us. It is to be able to say, "All I know is this: once I was blind, now I can see" (John 9:25). It is to have done with strenuous exercises of mind and body as means to discover God, and to find oneself already where those exercises were meant to bring us. It is, in short, to have received as a gift what some men spend their lives fruitlessly seeking: an at-one-ness with the Ground and Source of all that is, with that divine Mystery who remains a mystery even though we exultantly learn to call him "Father."

But why was Jesus seen as the bringer of such a gift? During his life he had troubled or delighted people with his teaching, but he had not evoked the response we are describing. At his death his disillusioned and fearful followers had fled, wanting nothing more than to sink into a safe obscurity. Even at his trial the stouthearted Peter had denied knowing him. What changed all this?

Here we come to the event that can only be received as the most embarrassing or the most liberating item of Christian belief. Jesus was dead. His friends had seen it, the authorities had certified it, and if there had been any possibility of trickery about the matter, his contemporary enemies would have done a far more effective job of tracking it down than any present-day sleuth can hope to do. Then he was alive again—evidently different, yet essentially the same.

Incredible. Superstitious. Impossible. Even in rather poor taste. His followers themselves would have agreed, and resisted the idea (Thomas refused to believe such nonsense: "Unless I see the mark of the nails on his hands, unless I put my finger into the place where the nails were, and my hand into his side, I will not believe it," John 20:25). Others scoffed at unlikely tales being told by women (Luke 24:22). But at last

---

‡ All New Testament quotations are from *The New English Bible* unless an asterisk is added to the reference; those so marked are my own translation. Old Testament quotations will usually be from the Revised Standard Version.

the men who had been terrified stepped out into the streets to proclaim the scandalous news (scandalous in that day no less than in this!) that God had raised Jesus from death. Many of those men accepted persecution and execution rather than recant this intolerable absurdity.

How it had happened, the friends of Christ did not pretend to know, but *that* he had been dead and was alive again meant for them that nothing could ever be the same again, and Jesus, their old friend and teacher, had become their Christ—the God-sent one.

The resurrection of Jesus was at once God's endorsement of his work, and the necessarily unique, authoritative event designed to shock us out of the conventional religious grooves so that we become aware that not rationality, mysticism, ritual, nor magic can bring us, unaided, to the most important truth of all: this comes from beyond us and it comes as a gift.

It will not do, as some have done, to reduce this difficult Easter event to a mere "resurrection of faith" in the disciples of Jesus. This renewal of faith occurred, obviously, but why? The resurrection of Jesus remains enigmatic, but no theory of mass hallucination and no "Passover plot" manipulation of the data will satisfy, I think, the serious and objective investigator. It is the rock on which we break or are built into vessels of new life and hope. It cannot be evaluated by conventional forms of historiology, for these operate by criteria which arbitrarily exclude it, since it is not repeatable and is like no other event in our experience. It is the event without which there would have been no Christianity, but only the memory of a minor preacher who was executed as a corrupter of important traditions.

The thing that is difficult to accept, but essential for Christianity, is the idea that what is historically possible is not to be measured by our usual standards. *Anything* is historically possible if it is possible to God, and the resurrection of Christ actually offers a clue to the final possibility of human history itself. It was a kind of re-creation, and as such it becomes credible if we begin not from the perspective of what is ordinarily experienced but from the acceptance of the God to whom Jesus constantly referred, the God who is the creator (out of nothing!) of the entire system of processes we call life and the universe. Now the possibility emerges that instead of declaring the resurrection impossible because it is unique in history, we must begin to see the meaning and possibilities of history as defined by the resurrection! He who created can create anew even in the face of the distortion of processes, the disarray of order, and the end of life itself.

But what Christians claim about the resurrection makes sense only if it is understood that this event was a part of a total, unique phenomenon which is the entire Christ-life with its teachings, actions, death, and new life. The resurrection gives new significance to the whole, but is itself made meaningful by the rest. Such is the importance of the resurrection that Paul admits: "If Christ was not raised, then our gospel is null and void, and so is your faith" (I Cor. 15:14). But it is the *whole* that is important, for after the resurrection it is seen that in some way this life lived by Jesus was the bearer of a self-disclosure of God.

The precise nature of the relationship of Jesus to God is a difficult theological issue—fortunately beyond the scope of this book! But at least we must record the basic convictions that Jesus was no ethereal sprite, no "heavenly being," but a man. He talked about God and a Kingdom of God (that is, a kingly rule of God within men) and as he spoke, lived, and died, God himself gave himself in freedom and love to mankind, calling all men to accept reconciliation with him and with the destiny for which they are intended. This coming of God to us is precisely the "Christness" of Jesus. One may say that the term "Christ" really refers to God's act of self-commitment to men, and it is because Christians find this act reaching them in and through Jesus, touching them to heal their estrangements and to overcome their lostness that they call him Jesus the Christ.

The Christ, then, embodied in Jesus, is God's Word to us and God's Act for us. It is the coming of the Beyond-to-which-we-belong to overcome our alienations and self-destructive pride. It is for this reason that Jesus has sometimes been called the Mediator: he repeatedly pointed beyond himself to God, claiming that the words he taught and the things he did were not simply his own. They were, as Christians came to believe, the necessary concrete point at which the Ultimate Reality communicated itself to men to give appropriate focus for man's mystical propensity and to indicate that history is no mere appearance, no illusion, and that matter and spirit are not alien to each other but that both are part of the creative process of God.

To "see" Jesus with the vision of understanding is to "see" God, not because Jesus is God (this he never claimed), but because in Jesus the *Christ*—the gracious self-declaring act of God—is present.

There is a sense, therefore, in which just as Zen likes to call itself the "school of Buddha's Mind" to indicate that its entire concern is to enable the adherent to enter into the state of awareness that the Buddha had in his enlightenment, so Christianity may be called the "school of Jesus' Mind." Paul says, "Be of the same mind as Christ Jesus (Phil. 2:5*), by which he means that Christians are to confront the world and each other from within an exciting awareness of the creative presence of God and to respond to that presence as Jesus did, in an attitude of joyful obedience, but an obedience in which they are prepared to defy conventions, to suffer outrageous rejections, and even to offer their lives if necessary rather than to truckle to establishments of right or left, or to worship any man, party, or nation.

To encounter a Christ, then, is to encounter at once a Word and an Act of the ineffable Ground of our being. This would be true wherever we genuinely found our Christ, even if it were true that different men met him differently embodied. But no one can meet more than one Christ, for such an event is so decisive for one's life and decisions that it precludes the very possibility of a repetition. It is such a recognition, I believe, that leads the author of The Letter to the Hebrews to say:

> For when men have once been enlightened, when they have had a taste of the heavenly gift and a share in the Holy Spirit, when they have experienced the goodness of God's word and the spiritual energies of the age to come, and after all this have fallen away, it is impossible to bring them again to repentance. (Heb. 6:4–6.)

For Christians, then, the Christ has been encountered in Jesus because in him alone do they find the extraordinary and sufficient signs of Christness—in his words, his actions, his character, his death, and his resurrection.

Jesus, then, is the embodiment of the Christ—the divine, illuminating, reconciling Word and Act. As John puts it, "The word [of God] became flesh and dwelt among us" (John 1:14*). John is writing in Greek and uses the Greek term *logos*, which means not merely "word" but creative intelligence and personal expression. Yet it is doubtful whether at its richest this word can quite convey the idea in the mind of the obviously Semitic writer. Rather, it seems to me, he may have been thinking much more nearly of the content of the Hebrew term *dabar*, which means "word" but which includes the idea that the word in question is no mere sound or symbol, but an entity which has a power to perform what it denotes. So, in Jesus comes a divine Word which is at the same time not merely an announcement of God's presence to men but the concretion of that presence itself. When Jesus says, "Anyone who has seen me has seen the Father" (John 14:9), he alludes to the fact that the man who feels himself grasped by the Christ knows the wonder, joy, and awe of finding himself in the presence of the ultimate Mystery.

We have said that Christianity is the "school of Jesus' Mind." It is now clear, however, that this will not be a sufficient description of it, for Jesus is not a repeatable phenomenon. A man, we have noted, can find his Christ in only one place, and now we must add that only one Christ can appear in the history of the world, for if there were more than one, they would not be the *Christ*. Other religions tell us of gods who re- peatedly appear incarnated in the world. Ancient religions tell us of gods who died every autumn and rose to life again every spring. But the Christ comes, as the Bible puts it, "once and for all at the climax of history" (Heb. 9:26) because he is *not* a manifestation of the cycles of nature, as were the ancient deities to whom I have referred, but of the God who creates nature but is not reducible to it. He comes, furthermore, only once because he is not only a Word from God but an Act in which God establishes *once and for all* the unchangeable, un- defeatable future and destiny of the cosmic enterprise. He is the Word about the end for which we exist appearing in the midst of our times and he is the Act by which God determines the channel through which the lost may find their destiny again.

Here, then, is the central, scandalous affirmation of Chris- tianity. A Galilean peasant dies the death of a criminal under Roman supervision and suddenly his life cannot be confined to Galilee but explodes into the world. And to ancient or modern men who ask, "Well, who was he anyway?" the Christian who has been amazed, discomforted, and thrilled by what he has found in him answers: "He is the definitive moment in the history of the world. He is the concretion in time and space of an attitude which transcends both because it is the attitude of God to his creation. He is the one who brings to us the promise of life and fulfillment, not by means of the subjective experience of tranquillity, but through struggle and suffering if necessary."

VIII

The Limit

(My God!) my God.
—*Gerard Manley Hopkins,*
"Carrion Comfort"

If Jesus as the Christ is to be seen as the Word and Act of God, before we begin to look for Christian answers to the problems raised in the first part of this book, we must briefly ask to what the word "God" seems to refer. After we have met the Christ, what can we say about God?

The first proposition of a Christian discussion of God is that he is undiscoverable to reason or any other unaided faculty of man. There have been many attempts to prove the existence of God, but to prove that anything exists is to place it as a necessary ingredient in some system of ideas or objects which is greater than it. Stars, for instance, have occasionally been shown to exist even before their discovery by a telescope because only their existence could account for the behavior of other, already observable bodies in space. But such a proof makes the proven star merely a part of an astronomical system. Similarly, "proofs" of God really reduce him to the role of a necessary part of a system of coherence which may require him but which also transcends him. He is thus necessarily finite and immanent. If a transcendent God exists, a God who is not merely part of some system but its mysterious Ground, he could not be demonstrated to exist by any chain of logic or any unaided intuitive experience. *Only his self-declaration could reveal him to us.* Consequently, any concept of the Ultimate which is entirely "reasonable" has little to do with the God of whom Christianity speaks. This is probably what Jean Daniélou means when he writes: "The One of Plotinus, the Brahman of Sankara, the Being of Spinoza, the absolute Mind of Hegel, are finally idols, not so much by being the object of reason as by being the sufficiency of reason." [29] Whether the One or Brahman are, in any sense, the sufficiency of reason is, of course doubtful, but Daniélou is probably trying to indicate that they belong to what a man can discover through his own resources.

Intuition (the immediate and total apprehension of some reality or conception) always brings with it a sense of assurance surpassing that even of persuasive logic. But it is also sometimes demonstrably mistaken, and it is most vulnerable when it turns its light upon questions of ultimacy. What can surely be intuited by anyone is the limited nature of our existence, our experience, and our awareness. We know what it means to be in a world we do not control, cast into a place in life as a shipwrecked sailor might be flung upon an inauspicious island. We did not determine our birth, and although we may delay our death a little, we cannot forever avoid it. In asking questions of life, our mind inevitably finds walls it cannot climb. Given this situation, we strive to understand the Limit surrounding us and, if possible, somehow to make that Limit part of us so that we overcome it by including it or by being included in it.

Whatever understanding we have of the Limit about us is shaped by analogies we draw from other, more examinable limits and apply to the ultimate one which curtails our life. For instance, we all know something of such physical limits as walls and doors, and if we apply analogies from this to our existence as a whole, we tend to derive a materialistic philosophy which sees human possibility and confinement in terms of matter or the economic manipulation of matter. Again, we know something of what we may call "normative" limits—rules imposed upon us, claims entered against us, and so on, based on what are held as fundamental distinctions of true-false, good-bad, and a thousand other value discriminations. If we think of the ultimate Limit of existence in such terms, we derive a moralism or idealism as our determinative philosophy.

If, as Gordon Kaufmann has excellently pointed out in an essay "On the Meaning of 'God,'" [30] another kind of limit commonly experienced by us—*the personal*—is chosen for analogy, we derive yet a different sort of philosophy. Every day we meet the resistance of another will; we are often baffled by the elusive depths of meaning and intention which determine the actions of a friend or an enemy. There is no intrinsic reason why the ultimate Limit to our existence should not be personal rather than material or normative or organic, and if this is indeed the most appropriate analogy we can apply to it, another reason for the futility of our unaided efforts to know God becomes clear. I can never really know another person except as he reveals himself to me. I can be aware of him as a resistance; I can know something about him; I can subject him to psychometric testing; I can spy on him. In short, I can collect a very large dossier about him, but none of this will enable me really to know him with that immediacy, directness, and mutuality which is the richest kind of personal knowledge. I shall know some data: I shall not know *him*. He must make himself, his heart, his integrity, known to me if I am to penetrate beyond the superficial levels of objective knowledge which satisfy psychology or sociology but which can never satisfy the demand of our own depth for personal engagement. How much more must this impenetrability of the personal apply to the Ultimate Person who is beyond us not merely because he is personal but because he infinitely transcends every other experience we have of what the word "personal" means?

God is, then, undiscoverable until and unless he offers himself in some way to us, and every effort to uncover the final Reality independently of his self-giving is doomed to fall short of finding *him*. It is for this reason that the Christ is necessary both as the concrete, historical self-disclosure of God and as the symbol of his eternal willingness to be known.

A second observation about God largely follows from this first one. God is a creative Other whose relation to the universe is one of both transcendence and immanence.

There are two strong and typical tendencies of the human imagination which much mystical religion demonstrates. The first is to escape the complexities of the many by reducing reality to One. The second is to escape the limitations of our finitude by thinking ourselves to be the Limit itself. As early as the Pharaoh Akhenaton, however, in ancient Egypt there was a glimpse of another possibility. "He almost broke through the limits of the cosmological experience of the unity of all reality to the experience of an ultimate otherness in the divine, which the cosmological framework of his orientation could not contain." [31] What Akhenaton almost achieved, the prophets of Israel almost perfected: the experience of encounter with an Ultimate beyond the universe itself, although intimately involved in it, and beyond Time, although gathering Time into himself.

This Ultimate, who was given in the Bible many names but for whom the symbol "God" is among us the cheapened and familiar title, was therefore revered in the Judaic tradition (and later in the Christian and Islamic traditions) as transcendent. This does not mean that he is a distant, remote, unapproachable entity but that he is *other* in some fashion than the universe he fills with his presence, and his otherness has several characteristics.

In the first place, the God of Christianity is the creator of all that is "other" than himself. He has being or existence because it is of his very essence to exist; everything else, on the other hand, comes into being through his will. The Biblical phrase to describe the status of all that is not God is *creatio ex nihilo*— creation out of nothing. Now, this is not meant as a mystification, but as an idea pregnant with a joyful understanding of the meaning of the universe. It means that our life, our world, our time, are free gifts, truly free in at least one important respect: they are given an otherness that releases them from being mere objectifications of God himself. This means that what happens to us, and to every blade of grass, really happens. It is no illusion, no scheduled, fixed, determined pseudo event, for there is a gifted otherness about each particular thing which makes its life real, even if transient.

Secondly, the idea of *creatio ex nihilo* has always entailed for most Christians the recognition of human responsibility within a world in which they are at once at one with yet different from all other creatures. When, in the Genesis story of creation, God has created Adam (whose name is Hebrew for "man") he tells his newest creature that it is to have rule over the rest of creation. This does not mean that man is made free to do as he impulsively pleases with a world made expressly for his pleasure, but that it is his unique gift and responsibility to begin to become what he can be, and to facilitate also the perfecting and completing of a world whose creation is only *begun*, by exercising the functions of management. There is no suggestion here that man is somehow supranatural; he is part of nature, bound up with all that exists in a common destiny. But that destiny rests significantly on his management. If he begins to manipulate the resources of the world unwisely, destructively, selfishly, then the entire world is thrown into a state of chaos. Man and his world are in an important sense *one,* and each, in its incompleteness, works upon and helps to fashion the other. But to man is given a responsibility which his freedom makes possible and his developing rationality and capacity for decision make effective. That is why Paul, in thinking about the alienation of man from his fellows and from God, sees the entire universe as involved and suggests the powerful image of childbirth to capture the feeling he has of the imperfect and struggling state in which we find ourselves: "Up to the present, we know, the whole created universe groans in all its parts as if in the pangs of childbirth." And, "yet always there was hope, because the universe itself is to be freed from the shackles of mortality and enter upon the liberty and splendour of the children of God" (Rom. 8:22, 21). In other words, any promise of fulfillment that Paul detects for man is extended to the universe itself without which man is not to be "saved."

Thirdly—and implied in what has already been said—is the conviction that the particular entities of our pluralistic universe have their existence as part of the purpose of God. My separateness is not a misfortune that I must deny or overcome; it is willed, intended, and has a perfection to achieve. Being free, I can fail to assent to my destiny, or I can fail to recognize it. I can make myself and my interests central, as though the universe existed for me, but I cannot renounce my particular reality without becoming subject to illusion. I can become lonely, vulnerable, terrified. Or I can escape these states into the illusion that I am a Cosmic Self. But I can also stop trying to be other than I am, and find my place in the universe acceptable and possibly even joyful when I take my eyes off my self and become a spontaneous and natural response to the Giver of that universe. In short, because I am free, I can try to become God. But because I am not God, I can become free to rejoice in what I am.

Thus, it is not the abandonment of my particularity that Christianity teaches, but the perfecting of it. The curious thing is, however, that this perfecting cannot be done self-consciously (the idea of a "self-actualizing psychotherapy" has often been faintly amusing to Christians) but only when we are turned away from ourselves to something other which commands our loyalty and draws us into a self-forgetting structure of meaning. As Jesus remarked to his followers: "Whoever cares for his own safety is lost; but if a man will let himself be lost for my sake, he will find his true self" (Matt. 16:25).

It is, in other words, not the crushing of desire or the pandering to it that Christianity aims at, but the redirecting of desire. It is the learning to desire not what would inflate our egos, but what would serve a cause to which we have given ourselves and which transcends us without demolishing our particularity.

For Christians, the road to fulfilling ourselves is through the abandonment of ourselves to God. This entails the acceptance of our creatureliness and finitude, and instead of struggling for immortality, like a fish on the end of a line, to relax and be glad to be "caught" in the ineffable purposes of him who is bringing the whole creation to a moment of birth and fulfillment.

Fourthly, God's otherness means that he is not reducible to the status of an object that we can use. God is no cosmic slot machine pouring out whatever we can pay for. He is no ethereal rabbit's foot to be clutched in times of terror. And he is not the chairman of the board who can be dismissed if we do not like his policies. When we face him, we are not merely talking to our alter ego (or even our *altar* ego!) but to him who cannot be absorbed in us and who calls us to stand up in personal authenticity and accept the responsibility of being what we are. As we shall see, this makes the shape of an authentically Christian mysticism different from many other kinds (although akin to that of Judaism or Islam) and means that as we are free in relation to God, God is free in relation to us. No priest can precipitate the presence of God in a sacrament, and no exorcism can keep him away from the world. The proper image of the appropriate relation of God and man is, therefore, not that of the fetus in the womb, but of two figures dancing in joyful, if often imperfect, harmony.

God is the creator of the universe and, as such, transcends what he has made. In his transcendence lies the possibility of his freedom and ours, of the tragic failure of our lives and of their ultimate fulfillment through both sorrow and joy. Above all, if God is transcendent, neither he nor we can be reduced to the shadow of the other. To curse God, to spit in his face, to reject him utterly are tragic and terrible possibilities, but possibilities they most surely are.

But if the notion of *creatio ex nihilo* means that God is other than the creation, it implies also that God is never truly absent from it. On what does the existence of the cosmos rest? For Christian thought, the only answer can be: on God. Langdon Gilkey writes that creatures exist "only so long as God's creative act continues to give them being, for they do not generate their own power to be from themselves." Again, "the renewal of each creature in each succeeding moment of its existence is a victory of being over the non-being of temporal passage." [32] The man who is renewed to live a new day but who does not look beyond himself for the source of this renewal is like a surfer who has forgotten he is standing on a surfboard.

The New Testament expresses this immanence of God when it declares that "in him we live and move, in him we exist" (Acts 17:28). If this were not so, we would not live and move at all, for God is infinite and no "other" can exist which does not, in some sense, exist "in him." Yet when a man examines himself with candor he must see that there is much within himself that is not divine, and know that this represents a real alienation from the Source of his existence, even though this alienation cannot be ontological but moral and noetic. God, however, cannot be alienated from himself, nor can the rebellion of man be a mere case of divine indigestion. So the truth about the relation of God to man is one that can be described only when transcendence and immanence, otherness and participation, are both ascribed to it, and even then the description is far from perfect.

There is one further element in the Christian understanding of the transcendence of God that must be acknowledged. Different historical ages tend to view transcendence according to some problem or characteristic peculiar to each, and in a time when men felt themselves most rigidly and confiningly bound by nature it was inevitable, and perfectly proper, for the heart of the meaning of divine transcendence to be related to this. God, then, was "supernatural." That is, he was unbound by that which bound men. As its origin, he was "beyond" nature with its regularities and limits. Agrarian societies in the ancient

world achieved a version of transcendence by virtually making
their god or gods personify nature or exemplify its rhythms
triumphantly. So there were gods who died in the autumn and
rose in the spring. For such gods as these, there could be no real
history, for events—at least the essential ones—repeated themselves endlessly, and a circle rather than a line became the
symbol for Time.

As Mircea Eliade has observed, it was common to such
societies that men sought security by aligning themselves with
the gods who conformed to natural cycles without being simply
destroyed by them, and one way of achieving this alignment
was to find, in the time and space men occupied, a sacred time
and a sacred place in which the power of the gods entered our
sphere to sacralize it and confer on men the power also to
triumph over the processes of birth and decay.[33]

The Judeo-Christian tradition reaches back, not to an agrarian origin, but to a nomadic one, and this is extremely important for its central conceptions of life, time, history, and
God. The nomad was constantly moving, and when he con-
ceived of a god this god was moving also—moving ahead of
him to lead him to pasture and, hopefully, a future that might
be better than the present. There was a "promised land" ahead,
at least metaphysically. So for the nomad it is not a sacred
place and a sacred time, but a sacred future that is the focus of
his confidence (even if he also erects a tabernacle in the
desert and installs sacred places and moments within the
present), and "transcendence" means that God overcomes the
limitations of the present.

As the centuries passed, Christianity illegitimately adopted
much of the psychology of the agrarian people. Christians, too,
acquired a sacred place and time as of preeminent importance.
Usually the sacred place was the church on the corner of Main
Street, and the sacred time was eleven o'clock on Sunday
morning. This was where and when God was to be found; this
was where he impinged on all our space and all our time,
and our hope was that he would somehow from there sacralize

everything. The God of Israel and of Jesus, however, cannot be confined in a moment and a place. He is, as the Talmud somewhere says, "the place of the world, though the world cannot be called his place." Consequently, our churches have tended to become the ultimate profanities—birdcages for the Spirit of God!

The truer Christian view is that God is nowhere confined. There are no meaningful distinctions to be made between sacred and secular places, occupations, or times, but God, who is everywhere present, is present to lead us toward a future which is the fulfillment of our Now.

The paradigm of Christian attitudes to life must therefore be Abraham, who left the highly developed comfortable city of Ur (the reason is obscure and, in any case, irrelevant) to journey into uncertainty. As the New Testament puts it: "By faith Abraham obeyed the call to go out to a land destined for himself and his heirs, and left home without knowing where he was to go" (Heb. 11:8). The star leading the Magi to Jesus' makeshift cradle; the pillar of fire by night and the cloud by day leading the ancient Israelites through the desert to their destiny—these are symbols of a profound realization that God is a God who is continuously creating the future out of the present, taking the warped and difficult material which the freedom of man provides him, and bringing us not despite it but by means of it to a destiny as yet obscure to us but clear to him.

The Christian is, thus, one who has in the present "no permanent home, but . . . [seeks] after the city which is to come" (Heb. 13:14). He is a man of hope. But this hope does not lead him to abandon the present, but to live in it and to move in it, to rejoice in it and work in it, for it is the place through which God and he are moving together and the promised but undiscernible future already enlivens and lightens it with the joy of anticipation. The present can, and should, be savored like a good wine, but we must not try to hold it or it will turn to vinegar.

We are saying, then, that the transcendence of God, associated with his immanence, implies that the destiny of the world and, as a part but not the whole of it, the human adventure, is a process in which God and we together participate. But the goal is God's and it will mean our fulfillment as part of the ripening of his creative process. Jürgen Moltmann correctly writes:

> The God who reveals himself in Jesus must be thought of as the God of the Old Testament, as the God of the exodus and the promise, as the God with "future as his essential nature," and therefore must not be identified with the Greek view of God, with Parmenides' "eternal present" of Being, with Plato's highest Idea and with the Unmoved Mover of Aristotle.[34]

God's transcendence means most importantly for us that he transcends our present even while he is immanent in it, and he holds the future in his hands even though he will not achieve it outside our activities. There is a promised land, but Abraham must go, dirtying his feet on the desert highways: it will not fall from the skies around him.

God is Truth. This is a sentence common to many religions, but in Christianity, as in Judaism before it, it has a special meaning which is required by some of the things we have already said. The Truth that is God is not precisely the truth of a correct syllogism; it is not quite what the Greek meant by *alētheia* or the Roman by *veritas*. Both of these refer to something that can be "unveiled" and made clear, while God remains always Mystery. The Hebrew word *emet* means truth of a somewhat different sort, its root referring to the idea of support. Jean Daniélou offers: "Thus (*emet*) means the pillar on which a building rests; it refers to the support that a child receives when resting in his mother's arms. . . . [When applied to God] it will designate Him as the one on whom man can lean with all his weight because He is true and faithful." [35] Thus, the Truth that God is, is not appropriated by reason or intuition but by faith, by trustful commitment of oneself, and it means that God fulfills his purposes and can be relied upon to bring the universe to the end for which he created it.

God is love. This sentence is not so common among religions, although I would not claim it as unique to Christianity. God is transcendent, then, but his transcendence does not preclude a sort of intimacy, for the God who speaks the Christ-Word is one who is continually limiting himself (to speak metaphorically) in order that man's otherness may survive and that man may be available as authentically personal, able to relate in free decision—the only kind of relationship that can satisfy the deepest character of love. Such love seeks men, suffers in them and for them, rebukes them, but never abandons them or coerces them into obedience. It can wait, and its patience is infinite. The God who is love is *One;* he speaks his word and performs his reconciling Christ-Act in Jesus; he is experienced by us in his living presence which, for convenience, we call the Holy Spirit. Here we have the heart of that most misunderstood of all Christian doctrines, the concept of the Trinity. This doctrine means that God's otherness is real, but not an absolute distance because he is never really absent from us even when he is absent from our awareness: he comes constantly and he came uniquely in the Christ.

But if God is continually present to us, the idea of his otherness warns us that we must not imagine that we own him. Martin Luther mocked certain enthusiasts of his day because, as he colorfully put it, "they pretend to have swallowed the Holy Spirit, feathers and all!"

There are, of course, many more things that Christians have said about God, and even if we eliminate the incredible quantity of sheer nonsense, there would be enough to fill many books the size of this one. What has been said so far, however, will be sufficient for our purposes and I will conclude this chapter by returning briefly to themes already discussed, in order now to conclude them in a way not quite possible before.

God is other than ourselves, although we cannot exist without his constantly renewed sustenance. Because he is not to be identified with our "depth" or our subjectivity or our essence (although all these things exist in him), we cannot begin to know him by introspection or by surveying the world about us, but only as he gives himself to us. It is true that the more we grasp of his Word and respond to his Act in Jesus the Christ, the more we are likely to find him expressing himself and giving himself in everything. But there is a place to begin responding to him, and that place is the Christ.

It follows that even our human propensity for mystical experience must be humbled before it can enter the service of Truth. We must be made aware that mysticism is wanton, freely giving itself to many masters (which, however, all sound like One when the mystic describes them), and the pride which would direct our mystical sensitivity to the object most pleasing to our self-esteem (because it is the object with which we can readily imagine ourselves identified and thus exalted) must be broken. Only when we have been thus wounded can we be healed and made ready to encounter the true God whose living presence in and among us is generally referred to in the Bible as his Spirit. Of this Spirit, Jesus once said: "The world cannot receive him, because the world neither sees nor knows him" (John 14:17). By this I find implied that not empiricism ("seeing") nor either naked intuition or rationalism ("knowing") are the avenues through which God's presence comes to our awareness, but that *faith* or childlike trust of which Jesus spoke so often.

There are three great paradigms of Judaic and Christian mysticism in the Bible that deserve much attention. In the first, the prophet Isaiah tells of a day when, standing in the Temple, he seemed suddenly to see it filled with heavenly creatures at whose center was the Lord God himself. The prophet writes: "And I said: Woe is me! For I am lost; for I am a man of unclean lips, and I dwell in the midst of a people of unclean lips; for my eyes have seen the King, the LORD of hosts!" (Isa.

6:5). Here the sense of the presence of God does not issue in a feeling of unity, a feeling that the mortal has been gathered into the immortal, but in a sense of radical and discomforting otherness. Only after this is comfort given and the experience of being made clean and whole—but still other! There is intimacy of a sort, but not the removal of mystery, and emphatically not the dissolution of the particularity of Isaiah.

The second of our examples is recounted in Luke's Gospel, and involves a strange story of a night of unsuccessful fishing by Simon Peter and a few colleagues. Jesus appeared at last, and after reluctantly following his advice, Peter actually takes a netful of fish. At this point Peter becomes aware that he is in the presence of someone other than a mere man like himself, and his first reaction is to fall to his knees and to exclaim, "Go, Lord, leave me, sinner that I am!" (Luke 5:8). Here again, the moment of enlightenment is followed immediately by the recognition not only of otherness but of the need for forgiveness and healing.

Finally, Luke tells us, this time in the book called The Acts of the Apostles, about the conversion to Christianity of the formerly hostile Pharisee, Saul (later to become known as Paul). Saul is actually on an expedition to uproot a company of Christians and arrest them when, like Isaiah but this time on the open road, he appears to have a sort of vision and hears a voice. Saul temporarily loses his sight and this is a clear symptom of a fairly classical kind of hysteria, but this should not blind *us* to what is important in the story. The result of Saul's experience is, at last, a complete reversal of the direction of his life and a continuing mysticism so intense that at times he can say, "For to me life is Christ" (Phil. 1:21), yet never the shattering of his awareness that he is a mortal man who, if he ever acquires immortality, will do so as God's gift, not as his essential or inherent right (Acts 9:1–31; I Cor. 15:53–57).

Again, since the lostness of men without God cannot be overcome except as God finds them, Christianity is not, in the ordinary sense, a "religion" at all. It is the response to being found. Its book, the Bible, "bears witness to a revelation of God addressed to men of all religions." [36] The revelation of which it speaks calls men to the humble acceptance of God's acceptance of them, and to an openness to the future and to a hope for the ultimate establishment of that divine purpose for all creation which is symbolized in the Bible by the phrase the "Kingdom of God." For Paul and the other early Christians, this was a new and strange kind of hope, for they had much to complain of in a land occupied and dominated by the mighty power of alien Rome, and little enough cheer to foresee in their future. But the coming of the Kingdom, in God's time, was the heart of Jesus' message, and they came to believe in it because it referred to the culmination of God's creative purpose, and the God who had raised Jesus from death could raise even a wasted, desolate, and despoiled earth to the glory he intended it to have. They knew themselves to be still bound to suffering and death, but now they found it possible to give themselves to these when necessary with a certain joy (as well as very real pain!), not because they enjoyed them—indeed, as far as human ingenuity and faithfulness to their work as Christ's men permitted they resisted them—but because even death can become a tool through which God mysteriously builds his Kingdom.

Here, then, is the heart of that experience and discovery which the word "Christianity" ought to mean. Now we must ask what relevance can be found here for the problems and struggles of our day.

IX

Christian "Being in the World"

> What a piece of work is a man!
> —*Shakespeare,*
> Hamlet, *Act I, Scene ii*

Christian answers to most of the problems of human experience or, for that matter, to problems of any kind so long as they relate to the universe, derive from an appreciation of the purposive creatorship of God.

For many people, the Biblical idea that God created the universe is a cause of difficulty. Has science not told us that the world could not have been fashioned in a mere six days? Can we believe that, as Genesis tells us, the Lord created light and daytime before he created the sun which we know to be the source of light for our part of the cosmos? How can we reconcile the fossil record of patient ages, and the apparent process of evolution with the first chapters of the Bible?

The simple truth is, there is no need to reconcile these things. The Bible is quite cheerfully prescientific and uses the terms and concepts available to its writers in their time to discuss something that is not within the domain of any science. Science is concerned with the relationships between finite objects within space and time, and in this realm of discourse the Bible is no rival; on the other hand, the idea of God's creatorship refers to the more fundamental problem of why there are such relationships and such objects, why there is either space or time, and the value and meaning of all these things. A scientific discussion of the origin or creation of the world would deal with the process by which things came to be as they are, but a theological discussion leaves all this aside, except accidentally, until it has examined the absolute ontological dependence of all things and processes upon an infinite Originator. "The myth of creation does not tell us about a first moment of time, any more than the myth of the Fall tells us about a first human being. What it does tell us is that every moment of time, like every contingent thing, comes to be from the creative power of God." [37] In short, there *is* a universe because the infinite Mystery who has presented himself to us in the Christ intends that there shall be; its existence is part of his purpose and design.

Already a few clear implications of the idea of creation must be obvious. First, the doctrine of God's creativity means that whatever exists in our experience is finite, contingent, and could not sustain itself in existence without the supportive power of God. Second, whatever evil, malignancy, or misery there may be, in essence the universe is at least potentially coherent and "good." In this, Judaism and Christianity find themselves violently opposed by a considerable number of opinions. In many systems of thought, for instance, there is a basic dualism, and the cosmos is seen as fundamentally divided between good and evil roots. In many ancient Eastern myths a God or Principle of Order originally subdues a monster who represents disorder or death and constructs the world out of the ruins of his victim. In certain versions of Zoroastrianism a beneficent God constructs whatever is good, but this is matched by a malignant spirit who creates all that is harmful in the world. To turn to more modern times, Edgar Sheffield Brightman and Alfred North Whitehead both had systems in which God was eternally matched with something other than himself, so that real or apparent ambiguity in the resultant universe is explicable. In all such views God is finite, and if his partner is eternal evil, it is inevitable that evil becomes a virtually ineradicable element in the totality of things. Against ideas of this sort Christians affirm that God is infinite and his creation essentially good, and that therefore the evil in it, however real and terrible, is derivative and conquerable. To this idea we shall have to return later.

If dualism tends to leave us with a world that is partly evil by nature, most forms of monism (another of Christianity's great and ancient rivals) or pantheism tend to an opposite view. Here *only* God—the One, the Absolute—really exists and anything that cannot be God can, consequently, be no more than an illusion of some kind. So man is comforted by the assurance that evil is not real (sometimes ingenious phrases such as "negative goodness" are invented for it) and that he himself, "deep down where it counts," is divine. Against this, Christians affirm that evil is no dream, no mere illusion, but a terrible and destructive presence; and man is emphatically not God. When one considers the range of behaviors in which men feel themselves "reinforced," it seems clear that there is a discontinuity between men and God, whatever kind of continuity there may also be; and anyone who is suffering from the needle-pointed inhumanity of man (exhibited in splendid ingenuity from ancient thumbscrews to modern death camps) is little comforted by the idea that evil is not real. Indeed, if he finds a colleague who has accepted this idea, he is likely to envy the latter's capacity for escapist self-persuasion.

In dualism there is a failure to take with full seriousness the authority of God; in monism there is a failure to credit the particularity of the individual. We have not tried to prove that either view is incorrect, but have said that Christianity takes a middle path between them, affirming at once the power of God and the integrity of man, for the latter is created to be real and, in large measure, self-shaping and thus capable both of inflicting and suffering real pain. Even such inescapable trials as old age, disease, and death are real; but they are unmitigated misery only under certain very common circumstances which are in no way necessary. To this also we must return later.

The notion of God as supreme Creator means also that he, and he alone, lays an ultimate claim upon us and he alone is the source of meaningful judgment, compelling promise, and ultimately restoring love.

After these few generalizations about the more obvious implications of God's creativity, we must turn to other, less obvious ones, the discussion of which will at times require expansion of the points we have already made.

"The universe arises through the will of God." Every word in this sentence is clear, yet its meaning is forever extending beyond our grasp, for the better we understand it, the more clearly we see it as the expression of mystery. The mystery is impenetrable, yet it touches with illumination every facet of our lives. The question of the *manner* of the world's creation is largely irrelevant to many Christians, but the fact that all that is exists only as willed and constantly sustained by God is the fundamental Christian datum. And when the God is envisaged as he whom Isaiah trembled to confront, as the mysterious Other who is imperfectly but commandingly presented in the Bible, and who, without ceasing to be Other, is nevertheless closer to us than our breathing: when *this* God of infinite majesty is seen as the creative and single Ground of existence, one is suddenly aghast that men ever thought themselves the center of things. Why did it ever occur to men that the world existed for their benefit? What is clear in the Bible, and makes sense to Christian experience, is the conviction that the universe, *including man,* exists for God and for a purpose of his which can never be more than partly comprehended by us. Nor is man that work which alone really matters, everything else existing as adjunct to him. Man has a destiny under God, but so has the whole created order, and these individual destinies combine to form a whole, but no part is simply trivial and no part enjoys all the divine concern. This is clearly suggested by Paul in the eighth chapter of Romans where man is placed in relation and continuity with the universe and the affirmation is made that the fulfillment of human destiny will mean the simultaneous fulfillment of the cosmic destiny, since all creation is bound together in one purpose which is the "child" our laboring universe struggles to bring forth.

In short, the process of creation is continuing even in our day, but now a new word is applicable to it: salvation. Part of the method by which the creation is presently effected is the freedom of man. Without a capacity for decision and some measure of individual and collective self-determination, man would evidently not become the fulfillment of God's purpose. But with these elements in his making he turns himself away from God, seeking fulfillment in his own intentionality, seeking the Ultimate in his own depth, and the divine creativity must therefore proceed as simultaneously a restoring of man and a healing. Nowhere has our human condition been more picturesquely described than in the fascinating story of the building of the Tower of Babel—a story, alas, traditionally wasted in our culture on the very young, who have no hope of penetrating its central core of meaning.

> Now the whole earth had one language and few words. And as men migrated from the east, they found a plain in the land of Shinar and settled there. And they said to one another, "Come, let us make bricks, and burn them thoroughly." And they had brick for stone, and bitumen for mortar. Then they said, "Come, let us build ourselves a city, and a tower with its top in the heavens, and let us make a name for ourselves, lest we be scattered abroad upon the face of the whole earth." And the LORD came down to see the city and the tower, which the sons of men had built. And the LORD said, "Behold, they are one people, and they have all one language; and this is only the beginning of what they will do; and nothing that they propose to do will now be impossible for them. Come, let us go down, and there confuse their language, that they may not understand one another's speech." So the LORD scattered

them abroad from there over the face of all the earth,
and they left off building the city. (Gen. 11:1-8.)

Like most stories that speak of God and man, this one is
not perfect. Its suggestion of a somewhat petulant deity
knocking down his rivals' blocks can hardly be regarded as
adequate, but the point of the story is actually man, not God,
and in this respect it is superb. What is suggested is that man
is himself a creative being (part, at least, of what is meant
when it is said that he is created in God's image), but that he
is not content to build his city *under* God: he must go farther
and reach into the heavens themselves, there to occupy the
place of God. He is not content to be *given* a name, but must
"make a name." This is the essence of pride, and the consequence is that men are not satisfied to become collectively
their own God, but next begin to become individual gods,
each with his own frame of reference, his own inviolable values,
his own puissant interests—in short, his own "language," which
is unintelligible to others and which separates and alienates
him from them. This consequence is the natural result of pride,
but it is also a judgment of God upon the efforts of man when
those efforts separate humanity from its true belonging and
becoming, its proper destiny and glory. *Man's* creativity is to
be a part of *God's,* not a rival to it.

This ancient story is, then, an analogy upon which the
divisiveness of modern self-interest, of nationalism, class-con-
sciousness and racism, and all other manifestations of pride are
to be understood. It is an image of today's so-called "Youth
Culture" as well as of today's "Establishment," since the actions and outpourings of both are heavily laden with indica-
tions of arrogance, but it is especially an image of today's
human culture which is so infected by pride and the attempt
to displace God that it is breaking up almost exactly as the
people in the story of Babel did—splitting into groups which,
as we say, "cannot communicate" because each is obsessed
with its own "words" and considers it a virtue not to feel the
significance of those of any other party. It is amusing to hear

the adult generation accused by youth of "hypocrisy" when so many young people are "doing their thing" at the expense, if not of their parents, at any rate of a "straight" society on whose flesh they live as parasites. And it is amusing to hear the youth accused of irresponsibility by an older generation whose amazing disregard for consequences has brought upon us a pollution of the air, sea, and land that may already be irreversible. The fact is, our "enlightened self-interest" has never been remarkable for its enlightenment and the consequences of groups and individuals seeking to become their own centers of value, their own "gods," is exactly that imaginatively pictured by the Tower of Babel story. Let no one read that and, looking around at the world today, say that the Bible is irrelevant!

Of course, if Christianity demands that our pride be set aside, that the first step toward God and toward our own fulfillment is the step into the humility which laughs at our own pretensions, our own rhetoric, and sees us as mere tadpoles pretending to be toads, it is not likely to be vastly popular. Rather than turn to this, we will invent or discover another religion more flattering to our ego or more amenable to our desire for personal transcendence and power. The religion most likely to succeed in our day is the one that is a symptom of our sickness, not its cure: the religion that is itself a building of a tower by which we climb to God's place, not one that promises first to break our pride and *then* to make us rejoice to be in our own place and to find that place an unexpected glory.

So the continuing creativity of God today must partly take the form of healing us. But his ointment is love, and his strength is patience, for if freedom is an essential part of what he wills us to be, he cannot cure us by force. This is the point of the parable of the lost son recounted in the fifteenth chapter of Luke's Gospel. The young man had demanded, and received from his father, his share of the family property and had gone off to make his fortune. Things did not go well, however, and he found himself at last without money or friends, having to support himself by work that no one else wanted to do. Finally, his desperation is the tool that cracks the hollow shell of pride, and he begins to see himself more realistically. He turns tortured and reluctant steps toward home, but before he reaches it his father rushes out to meet and rejoice with him. The loss of the money, the wasted years, are irrelevant. What matters now is that love can begin to heal because the young man is willing to be healed. There is no blame from the father, for blame is irrelevant too. All that matters is life lived in love and lived fully—lived toward a destiny that is above small-minded personal pride and that has had to wait until such pride fell under the weight of its own folly.

So God waits. But when a man sees through the shallowness of his pride and turns toward home he finds that the Christ was precisely that rushing toward him of the God who will not force him to accept sanity, but joyfully accepts *him* when he wishes to be sane.

There are radical injustices in our world, because it is easy for dominant groups to use other groups and persons as blocks with which to build their own Babel. We mount higher toward our chosen heaven upon the broken bodies of the dispossessed, the underprivileged. Finally, revolution comes, as it must, but it does not cure what is really amiss, for it merely substitutes a new lot of broken bodies for the old ones, and the new heaven (whether it be called a classless society or Utopia) already has the stench of drying blood.

We ask: How is justice to be found? How can imperfect beings fashion a political system in which the hell of inequity is at least made cool enough to be tolerated? How can nations learn the arts of peace and forget those of war? We would like a simple, practical answer—something we can begin to put into effect immediately. But Christianity knows no such answer. Indeed, it knows that there is no such answer. But it knows a way that we might follow and an image that might go before us like a star. It is the way of painfully recognizing the futility of pride and of seeking to bring ourselves and our fellows into an allegiance to the God who recognizes no social classes, who patronizes no particular age group, and to whom the nationalistic war cries of this day are as unmoving as those of the ancient Philistines. And its image is of a society made classless not by bloody struggle, but by surrender to that One to whom each man is intrinsically important.

This is the secret of community. Community does not arise because we cunningly employ the artificial devices of group dynamics or sensitivity training, or because we "plan" it (with a convenient shopping center in the middle and churches at each corner), but because a number of persons find a common loyalty stronger than their egocentric differences. A universal community would demand an object of loyalty of universal proportions. It is the attainment of such community around the one Center appropriate for us that is meant by the Biblical phrase the "Kingdom of God," and this is the vision in the enraptured mind of Isaiah when he wrote:

> He shall judge between the nations,
>   and shall decide for many peoples;
> and they shall beat their swords into plowshares,
>   and their spears into pruning hooks;
> nation shall not lift up sword against nation,
>   neither shall they learn war any more.
>   (Isa. 2:4.)

But the mark of the terrible depth to which our pride runs in us is the fact that religion itself, and distortions of Christianity, have become excuses for war! There is no hope until we forget religion and allow ourselves to be found by God.

In short, sick men build sick societies, and the unjust placidity of today's old order as well as the shrieking of revolutionary dogmas are alike symptoms of a sickness that will infect *any* new order we construct. Such an observation may not be popular but it will appear irrelevant only to those who are obsessed by a vision that is itself irrelevant because devoid of an awareness of our lostness.

If human society is disordered by our pride and egocentricity, so is man's relation to his natural environment. Here, again, the cure offered by Christianity is the possibility of our reconciliation with a God who transcends nature itself, for reconciliation to him forces us to recognize that what is not human is not therefore merely at our disposal. If nature, as much as man, is God's creation and has a destiny, then the despoiling of it is an assault upon the heavens, an attack upon the God to whom nature is a child beloved.

When, in the first chapter of Genesis, God is represented as giving man mastery over the natural order, this does not mean that man may indiscriminately abuse the resources of the world. It means, as we have said, that man is that part of nature upon whom is laid the burden and the privilege of managerial responsibility, of creatively working as an element in the divine creativity to accomplish the final purpose of God in the perfect establishment and ordering of things.

In the face of our patent capacity to destroy or to help the processes of nature it is easy to understand man's arrogance, which leads him to eliminate natural species and ravish the land and water of his planet. But what is called for is, rather, a sense of wonder and awe that such power should have been given him. This is expressed magnificently in the Eighth Psalm:

When I look at thy heavens, the work of thy fingers,
    the moon and the stars which thou hast established;
what is man that thou art mindful of him,
    and the son of man that thou dost care for him?

Only when one has thus been humbled by the grandeur of that natural order in which we are so small a part may we, with appropriate astonishment, gratitude, and devotion to both God and nature go on to say:

Yet thou hast made him little less than God,
    and dost crown him with glory and honor.
Thou hast given him dominion over the works of thy hands;
    thou hast put all things under his feet,

all sheep and oxen,
  and also the beasts of the field,
the birds of the air, and the fish of the sea,
  whatever passes along the paths of the sea.

When this is seen not as signifying man's omnipotence but his responsibility and the incredible honor he has of sharing in God's creative work, the next stage is not to cry, "Glory to Man in the highest, for Man is the Master of things!" Rather, one must whisper:

O Lord, our Lord,
  how majestic is thy name in all the earth!

Mankind's true glory, then, is to participate in the continuing creativity of God, establishing a perfect order in nature and in human society; but instead, we have become ambivalent in our work, creative here, destructive there, for we have lost ourselves in ourselves, and God's continuing creation of *us* requires therefore that we be found by him and restored to a true vision of ourselves. We are not, as some have held, an aberrantly rational creature cast into a meaningless world, like a man lost in an enormous building full of locked doors which his one precious key will not open. We are creatures whose proudly distorted rationality is designed to be part of the process by which the intelligibility and order of the universe are perfected and brought to light. But a lost man can neither understand the meaning of such order as he sees nor extend it as he should.

The creativity of God and the action of God in Christ to save man from his lostness and alienation are therefore not really two events but one, for the rescuing of man from his radical disorientation toward inappropriate belongings and destinies is essential to the fulfillment of God's purpose.

Once we have seen a glimpse of the relation of man's creative potential and God's in even the vague and tentative way we have outlined here, an approach to the meaning of some recent developments in science and technology begins to appear. Since the whole order of things under God constitutes his creation, and since man's ability also to create is contained in this, whatever we can do shares, at least potentially, in the creativity of God and may move toward his purpose. Thus, for instance, the possibility that a man may be able to combine the necessary elements and construct life in a test tube is no theological dilemma. If I should ever meet a man whose mother was a glass jar, I shall know that he too is one for whom the Christ came; he is as much a man whose existence is part of the *creatio* of God as anyone. (Nevertheless, the conventional method of reproduction, although old-fashioned, retains unique satisfactions!)

Similarly, the possibility of genetic engineering and of correcting by drugs, electrodes, or conditioning unconstructive modes of human behavior may be seen as, in principle, a possibility within man's derived creativity and as therefore also potentially contributing to the purposes of God.

However, our understanding of the lostness of men raises a very serious question about the actual application of methods of behavior control or of genetic manipulation of the species, for such enterprises, like all others that men undertake, will be impregnated by our prideful alienation and inevitably become the building of a new kind of Babel. Those who select the "acceptable" behaviors, and those whose criteria determine the procedures of the constructive geneticists are themselves distorted beings whose acceptance of such responsibility should be agonizingly difficult. The man who is *eager* to prepare the blueprint for future generations is likely to be a very dangerous man indeed.

We have said that God does not coerce us into accepting him because it is evidently part of the delicate "becoming" of mankind that we be free, in some measure, to determine our own individual life-style. Now we must explore this point a little more because it has vital implications for our manipulation of the behavior or genetic construction of others.

The word "free" has been used several times in recent pages, and a clear implication of all that has gone before is that the optimal man is one who freely shapes his life. Now we must ask what this highly ambiguous word means in the context we have provided for it.

First of all, let us note that it does *not* mean that a free man's behavior is uncaused; that would be chaos, not freedom. Nor does it mean that there is open to us some sort of absolute freedom in which we could literally do anything. There are various factors which condition our existence, among them being the sheer givenness of our biological constitution, the limitation of our intelligence, the restriction of our knowledge, and the formation of automatic responses through social conditioning. It makes no sense, therefore, to speak about "free will" as if there were a little oblong box labeled "will" inside us which kept itself pure and untarnished by all external influences.

At best when we talk about human freedom we are talking about relative degrees of ability to make decisions and choices from a range of possible behaviors. At one end of the spectrum a man may do whatever he does automatically and spontaneously without reflection because his responses are so narrowly conditioned that no options are really available to him. Such a man may *feel* free because he is without struggle and indecision, but such a man is little more than a piece of litmus paper. At the other end, a man may have to undergo hours of uncertainty as he considers various possibilities and tries to find a reason which accords with the values and goals he recognizes to be his own in order to justify his decision, knowing that this very struggle actually calls into question those values and goals themselves. In short, the unreflective man feels free; the wise man, in certain circumstances, feels great pressures and constraints but has a higher degree of freedom because he is aware of the pressures and of options for decision.

There are three factors involved in decision-making: the individual's centeredness or integrity, his perception of a range of options, and the pressures he feels from each of these options as a result of his former conditioning, his natural appetites, and his inclinations.

First, let us think about individual centeredness. In the Biblical story of the Garden of Eden the two persons, Adam and Eve, are pictured as roaming happily in a kind of paradise. Life is idyllic. There is no anxiety, no frustration. But in the middle of the garden is a tree from which the couple have been instructed not to eat. A naïve reading makes us wonder why this should be so, why God should plant a tree in paradise whose fruit poisoned the minds of his creatures with "a knowledge of good and evil." But, upon reflection, from our experience as human beings we can tell why this had to be so. Adam and Eve began existence in a state which Paul Tillich called "dreaming innocence," a state in which they were mere packages of potentiality drifting toward no destiny. To become authentic persons it was necessary that they make a decision about the direction and focus of their lives—that they be obliged to say yes or no about something quite determinative and final. Without the exertion of decision they do not begin to be self-affirming individuals, and without being that they cannot be that part of nature which God intends the distinctively human to be. So they are given a tree that is to force decision—obedience or disobedience. It would not be enough to refrain from eating its fruit simply because the idea of doing so never occurred to them. They must be confronted with the option of deliberately eating or deliberately refraining, and whatever their decision, they will, by deciding, have begun the tortuous road toward fully developed humanity. To decide *not* to eat means that they will still not make distinctions between "good" and "evil" because they have chosen obedience and their character will be grounded in the good which will have no name because it has no opposite against which to identify and name it. To choose to eat means that they will now have the knowledge of good and evil, that is, they will distinguish some actions as good and some as evil because their self-establishing decision happens to have led into an orientation which actualizes evil (disobedience) as it makes them lose the clarity of their potential relation to the point of origin and meaning for life. But even to decide for disobedience and lostness is better than to decide nothing; a lost human being can be found, but he who never becomes human because he continues to drift in the emptiness (which is not innocence) of characterless oblivion is neither lost nor found—he is not really alive.

The point of this superb myth is, then, that even though now expelled from the garden, Adam and Eve are truly *persons* and although the road ahead may be hard, there is hope for their future, for what is created can be re-created or renewed. They have learned to say "I" and they are therefore vulnerable. But they have also attained the possibility of relationship, including relationship with God. Love now stands as a human potency, for love is a relationship between an "I" and a "Thou" which does not dissolve or destroy either, but which causes each to become ever more authentically himself (since to be loved may be the most liberating of all experiences) while at the same time to be part of something transcending his individuality and overcoming his isolation.

It is the becoming an "I" that is meant here by the term "centeredness." I acquire a "center" as I become a coherent self. My center consists of those values which I come to accept, those perspectives and sentiments which define or demonstrate my "self-expression." I act "authentically" when I act in accordance with the values that constitute my "center" and inauthentically when I conceal or compromise those values. And among the values, if I am to be unambiguous, there should be one that draws the others into a coherent and hierarchical structure around it—a "dominant sentiment" as Gordon Allport calls it in a provocative book entitled *The Individual and His Religion,* or an "object of devotion" in Erich Fromm's terms, providing a frame of orientation for my life.

Such a centeredness is not necessarily final or irrevocable. It is one of the mysteries of human life that men occasionally do change their dominant sentiment and reject an old object of devotion for a new one. But to be without such a center is to be without any ground upon which to make major decisions, for it is to have no clear content in the word when we say "I."

The second element in serious decision-making is awareness of a range of possibilities. No decision is called for if there is only one line of behavior recognized by us that serves the values we hold to be ultimate. A man who knows who and what he is will act quite spontaneously in such circumstances, and the question of freedom or the lack of it does not even arise. But when we see an arc of possibility before us, we are free to choose to the extent that we are capable of recognizing the pressures each of the separate options exerts upon us, and to understand why we experience that pressure. The man who is governed wholly by his passions will accept the option that most passionately moves him, but what is probably uniquely human is the capacity to use our reason to understand both passion and appetite, to master, in fact, our blind inclination by subjecting it (painfully, no doubt) to rational evaluation in the light of what we hold to be valuable. One may finally choose a behavior that gives very little passional satisfaction, but that serves a value to which we have given the loyalty of our minds. Since rationality is a more or less distinctive attribute of humanity, *human* freedom means the strengthening of reason to the point at which it can engage our passion directively in determining behavior.

By reason too we can analyze the implications of other pressures that impinge upon us, whether societal or personal, and as we increasingly understand the forces and conditions that move us we become increasingly able to mitigate the blindness of our customary responses.

Every human action is indeed a response of some sort. But it is never a mere reaction to a discontinuous given. It is not, in other words, action after passivity. Stimulus and response overlap and there is interaction between them. If stimulus sets off response, response aims at modifying stimulus. Intelligent action seeks to understand what impinges on us, and more than that, to change it.[38]

Human freedom, then, means the understanding of what we do and why we do it, and the adapting of our actions to a reasonably appraised system of values.

The ultimate limit of our freedom appears in our capacity to recognize that the very value we have held as supreme is itself vulnerable to criticism and to displace it at last to the advantage of another, thus altering significantly our own "center" by a new supreme commitment.

Viktor Frankl has pointed out that under certain circumstances the human animal seems to lose both the will to pleasure and the will to power without losing the capacity to live, but that when a man no longer finds any ground to hope for the attainment of some sort of meaning in his life, life itself seems to be prejudiced.[39] In other terms we might say that a sense of living meaningfully is a powerful, if not the most powerful, source of reinforcement for men. If we ask why this is so, there seems little to say beyond the quite unhelpful observation that "it's the nature of the beast." Christians believe that man is created for a destiny which he can deny, but which never leaves him alone, and the will to meaning, the hunger for significance and fulfillment are, in fact, parts of the equipment with which he is endowed and without which he would not be completely human. Thus every form of pure romanticism is doomed to disappoint us, as is every attempt to achieve a total intellectualism. Man is that animal in which appetites, passions, and rationality must learn to work together for the joyful fulfillment of meaning, and man is "free" in the human sense of that word, to the extent that he understands his own actions and the influence on them of all that he is and all that impinges upon him, and to the extent that he consequently *chooses* his path amid a variety of options. He is most free, of course, whose reason, passions, and appetites legitimately combine in pursuit of a common objective, but until we learn to educate our emotions as we can discipline and inform our reason we shall often have to endure a dividedness within ourselves which, although it indicates a kind of bondage, is still the mark of greater freedom than simple pre-rational spontaneity.

This has been a long digression, but an important one because we can now return to the question of whether the control and manipulation of behavior in other persons is theologically justifiable or not. We have said that it could be regarded, *in principle*, as part of man's creative potential to be able to produce, by genetic and behavioral engineering, an optimal person. But it now becomes clear that an optimal human being, from a Christian viewpoint, is one who fully realizes in himself that leadership by *reason* of passion and appetite that enables him to be responsible—that is, to choose a course of action among alternatives and to estimate and accept the consequences of the choice. He must be the person whose very "center" is itself the subject of his reflection and who has perceived as real alternatives the variety of objects which present themselves to us as the claimants to our ultimate loyalty.

Under these circumstances, any manipulation of human behavior that does not produce a higher measure of what we have been calling freedom is illegitimate and must be rejected by the Christian as not contributing to the authentic destiny of man. If we were to produce people who considered the claims of God upon them and responsibly set those claims aside in favor of some other loyalty, we should have performed creatively. If we were to produce men who acknowledged God and did all the "proper" things, spoke all the "right" words, and had only "good" thoughts, but without the capacity really to make a meaningful decision, we should have reproduced the "Garden of Eden" situation illegitimately, for we would have accomplished a regression in the species to the state of "dreaming innocence," which may have been the beginning but cannot be the goal of the human adventure. One of the virtues of

bad child-raising is that, in rebellion, the child may actually
blunder to a sort of authenticity; and one of the latent horrors
of scientifically competent conditioning is that organisms which
ought to be human may become unreflective, heteronomously
programmed responders who do not even guess that anything
else is possible:

> Here comes the happy moron;
> He doesn't give a damn.
> I wish I were a moron.
> My God! Perhaps I am!

So far we have found, in the notions of the purposive creativity of God, and the freedom and creativity of man, important
keys to a Christian response to such problems as man's place
in and responsibility for nature and community, and his possibility of self-fulfillment. More serious for many persons than
these issues, because more personally pressing, are questions
arising from our transience and our susceptibility to suffering.

In a world allegedly created by a good God, why is there
pain? Why do the just and honorable find themselves afflicted
by disease and disaster as much as do the reprobate and out-
law? Surely in a good world, made by a loving deity, if there
were suffering at all, it would be exactly commensurate with
man's deserving. Unhappily, God seems to be concerned with
something other than a script for a television Western.

No Christian has ever thought he had a fully satisfying
answer to this problem. It must be remembered, of course, that
the world is not to be thought of as complete, but as in process
of being created and in its unfinished state there may be much
that appears inexplicable. When clay is molded by a potter,
then colored, and finally fired in a kiln, one imagines that if it
had consciousness, it might well be a little disgruntled about
proceedings; but the result is beauty and usefulness. Part of the
Christian's attitude to the suffering of the world is the hope
and conviction that out of it the Creator can weave a beauty in
the final product to which pain itself will have lent some color

CHRISTIAN "BEING IN THE WORLD"

and form. Certain it is that a person who has survived in spirit and body a life of challenge, suffering, and struggle may be a very different character from someone whose entire existence has been sheltered and whose every need has been instantly and painlessly met. If life is an end in itself, suffering is merely a misfortune, but if there is a yet unfulfilled purpose toward which our life is moving, then there is ground to hope that the bitterest suffering may serve that purpose in some fashion. To believe or hope for this is to face our suffering differently, for, in Nietzsche's famous phrase, he who has a *why* to live for can endure almost any *how*. To say this is not, it must be noted, to say that any piece of suffering is deliberately planned and planted by God, but only that the possibility and actuality of suffering are ingredients in a process which transcends them.

Believing this, one may also believe that there is no condition of life in or through which fulfillment is not somehow served: "Whether a man finds himself in a concentration camp, in poverty, in sickness, or even facing death, he is no further thereby from what God asks of him for his own fulfilment." [40] This must have been in Paul's mind when he wrote:

> Five times the Jews have given me the thirty-nine strokes; three times I have been beaten with rods; once I was stoned; three times I have been shipwrecked, and for twenty-four hours I was adrift on the open sea. . . . I have met dangers from rivers, dangers from robbers, dangers from my fellow-countrymen, dangers from foreigners, dangers in towns, dangers in the country, dangers at sea, dangers from false friends. I have toiled and drudged, I have often gone without sleep; hungry and thirsty, I have often gone fasting; and I have suffered from cold and exposure. (II Cor. 11:24–27.)

The thing above all that sustains the Christian is the experience that even his affliction may be the ground upon which he is confronted by God. The magnificent poetry of The Book of Job recounts the inexplicable suffering of a just man who is driven to demand that God explain to him the reason for his torrent of afflictions. But when God comes, no explanation is given, yet the man is satisfied and exclaims:

> I had heard of thee by the hearing of the ear,
> but now my eye sees thee.
>
> (Job 42:5.)

And in the presence of God his question about suffering remains unanswered but undemanding. Indeed, inasmuch as it was the crisis of his suffering that broke the calm parade of his uneventful days and precipitated his quest for encounter with God it has become a source of benefit.

This does not mean that sickness and trouble are welcomed by the Christian. On the contrary, they are resisted and, if possible, averted or overcome. But in the belief in a transcendent purpose is the hope that nothing, not even our pain, is wasted in pursuit of the ultimate fruition of creation.

Beyond the other slings and arrows of outrageous fortune that belabor us, however, lies death, whose intransigence and inevitability make it the determinative boundary of almost all human hopes. Death isolates us as nothing else can, for whatever else we may do in company, each of us dies essentially alone, and this is nonetheless true if we are trampled to death by a horde of neighbors. How shall we overcome or be reconciled to this boundary and this loneliness?

One way of trying to conquer our anxiety about our own impermanence is to persuade ourselves that we are identical with some reality which transcends birth and death. This means denying the decisiveness of our everyday experience and taking refuge in a conviction or an experience of oneness with something which is in principle immutable and eternal. That such convictions, when honestly achieved, are comforting and that such experiences can be cultivated one need not doubt, but to many this road seems to demand the denial of too much.

Another way, on the whole less successful, consists of trying to achieve immortality *within* the realm of everyday life. Here we may attempt to identify ourselves with a cause or a program which we expect to live far beyond our own time and thus to provide for us an avenue by which we shall continue to have an effect in the future. We may talk about identifying ourselves with the great human experiment, and murmur into our wine that our immortality is the survival of the species. In the long run, however, this is no more satisfactory than other reachings for mundane immortality. The pyramids represent the boldest grasping for deathlessness in the ancient world, but they are today monuments to futility as they slowly erode under the assault of time and elements. And humanity itself, although it may survive for millennia, cannot hope to cheat the last oblivion.

Another of our devices is to pretend that death is in bad taste, and to ignore it until it occurs near us, and then to pretend that it is something else. So we produce a culture in which no one dies, although everyone at last "passes away" and the art of embalming (without the excuses prevalent in ancient Egypt) is dedicated to the proposition that every corpse will be a happy one. I look forward to the day when, after the fashion of some modern dolls, the dead shall be fitted internally with a tape recorder operated by a string so that with a tasteful flick of the wrist one may have them say, once again, their most memorable or most cherished phrases.

The first thing the Christian is bidden to do in the face of death is to recognize that it is real and that all his attempts to evade it are futile. Indeed, the fact that we must die should be seen as a revelation of the first truth which it is necessary for all of us to understand if Christianity is to be even a possible experience for us: the truth that *we* are not God, are not the Absolute, are not the Universe—are not anything but what we find ourselves to be in the face of death: a solitary, vulnerable, transient individual with only memory, reason, passion, and a sense of identity through the changes of the years to arm him.

When our stark and powerless singularity has become clear to us, then we are ready to understand the second great truth: that life is a gift to be received in wonder.

But when we have come this far, the question of God begins to be insistent. If I am not the source of my own power to be, is there such a source at all? If I am not God, is there a God? As Sam Keen has it: "The question of God is not the question of the existence of some remote infinite being. It is the question of the possibility of hope. . . . If God is dead, then death is indeed God." [41]

The root of the Christian conviction that death is not God, but that God is to be found even in the experience of death, arises from the perception that in the resurrection of the Christ, God has demonstrated his mastery, his victory, his transcendence over death itself and his capacity to conquer it in us. In the light of his resurrection, amazed disciples began to understand that just as the teaching of Jesus had been public, so his death and its aftermath were for Man. The resurrection was divine confirmation of the promise of fullness and fulfillment of life which Christ had voiced; it was a sign of the triumph of the creative intentionality of God.

That even the Christ must die, but that he is brought to a victory over death, means three things for men. First, it denies all pretensions we may entertain to an inherent immortality. We die. We are not immortal souls inhabiting corruptible flesh—this was not a Hebrew Biblical idea and became Christian only illegitimately through Hellenistic influence. Our glory and our hope are as participants in the purposes of God, and we can be joyful and fulfilled, therefore, only when we renounce the ambition to be gods and find our true belonging in God. We must learn not merely to present our lives in service to God, but to present to him even our dying, that both life and death—his gifts to us at first—by becoming our gifts to him are the free, willing blocks of which he builds his Kingdom.

Secondly, having put aside pretensions to immortal grandeur, we find that the perfecting of ourselves to which we are invited by the gift of life is the perfecting of our finite, limited, and partly conditioned selves. No matter what the Founding Fathers of the United States may have fondly believed, men are *not* created equal. But they are equally created for fulfillment in God's purposes, and the path to that fulfillment is the continuing development of their individual abilities and potential as these are continually offered to God. Indeed, ultimately it is the utter losing of ourselves in self-giving to God that is the curious means of our finding ourselves fulfilled. This is surely the significance of Tolstoy's splendid story *The Death of Ivan Ilyitch*, in which Ivan, a man whose life is described by Tolstoy as pedestrian, conforming to the unimaginative norms of his social class, discovers in his dying both the worthlessness of all that he has been or achieved, and that nevertheless in the absolute giving of himself, his life and death, to God he is liberated from triviality and meaninglessness. It must be admitted that to describe this experience is to fall easily into mere platitudes; but to *have* the experience of surrender and liberation is anything but platitudinous.

Thirdly, the Christ's death and resurrection mean for us that life is ultimately triumphant over death, but not because of any intrinsic quality in human life itself. The key to this victory is God, who weaves even the bizarre circumstances created by men into his progressing creation of a Kingdom. Being called into existence "out of nothing" and being sustained in it by God, an irrevocable and final alienation of ourselves from God could mean nothing but—literally—Nothing. It is in this sense—"obliteration"—that Paul uses the word "death" in his famous dictum: "Sin pays a wage, and the wage is death, but God gives freely, and his gift is eternal life" (Rom. 6:23).

In short, human alienation from God, if allowed to produce its appropriate end (its "wage"), would lead to the blankness of the final defeat of life, but the gift with which God negates negation is a renewal of life, and this gift has been made a recognizable prospect through Christ's resurrection. It is his confidence in the final victory of life and of God which is being expressed in Paul's irrepressible shout of jubilation:

> Then what can separate us from the love of Christ?
> Can affliction or hardship? Can persecution, hunger,
> nakedness, peril, or the sword? . . . I am convinced
> that there is nothing in death or life, in the realm of
> spirits or superhuman powers, in the world as it is or
> the world as it shall be, in the forces of the universe,
> in heights or depths—nothing in all creation that can
> separate us from the love of God in Christ Jesus our
> Lord. (Rom. 8:35–39.)

Death, then, which the New Testament calls "the last enemy" (I Cor. 15:26), is conquered even in us, not because we are intrinsically some undying essence, but because God, who called life to particular expression in us, wills life's triumph.

But what does this victory mean for individuals? Does it mean that the person who has my name, my memories, my inadequacies, and my distinctive features will survive as a self-conscious entity who will chat in a celestial coffeehouse about a trout caught in Colorado in 1971? Frankly, I have no idea. Does it mean that, as Teilhard de Chardin believed, we shall all somehow be gathered up into a Cosmic Christ, becoming One without losing identity? I do not even know how one could guess. Does it mean we shall be like the separate drops of water falling into an ocean—nothing lost except our individuality? God alone knows. What the resurrection of the Christ implies is that the life which finds temporary expression in me now, with whatever values it has gathered during the lamentably unprofitable years of a murky existence, shall triumph over all negation, including death. If God wills the survival of my particular consciousness, I am quite happy to go on being conscious. If he does not, whatever really matters about me will survive in the way he deems best, and that is enough to hope for. I shall not waste time building pyramids. That he who called me into being is not thwarted by my capacity to die but shall complete what he intended in me is all the precision of expectation I need. As usual, Paul has said it better and with greater verbal economy: "If we live, we live for the Lord; and if we die, we die for the Lord. Whether therefore we live or die, we belong to the Lord. This is why Christ died and came to life again, to establish his lordship over dead and living (Rom. 14:8–9).

The thing that makes death terrible, therefore, is alienation from God, and the other side of this alienation is self-centeredness or centeredness in something less than God.

In concluding this chapter we shall sharpen a little our observation about two key concepts for understanding the Christian appraisal of the present state of mankind and its environment: alienation and hope.

We have spoken about the lostness of men, and have said that this consists of their separation from the true focus of their belonging in God. We have said that pride is the most common name of the root cause of our alienation—we try to take the place of God in our own esteem and to become ends unto ourselves. This is all true, but it is not the whole picture. Associated with pride, perhaps as merely an alternative expression of it, is apathy—hopelessness, shoulder-shrugging resignation, and moral inertia. Jürgen Moltmann writes: "Temptation then consists not so much in the titanic desire to be as God, but in weakness, timidity, weariness, not wanting to be what God requires of us." [42] Ordinarily we fluctuate between pride and apathy, but both are to be regarded as the marks in us of that condition of estrangement from God which is still sometimes called by its old-fashioned name: sin. We are alternately Prometheus, trying to snatch prematurely and in our own right what can be ours legitimately only as a gift, and Sisyphus, plodding away (even, perhaps, rather contented to be doing something) but without the fire and hope that would make his activity creatively human.

Out of illegitimate pride comes a host of derived evils: arrogance, hatred, oppression, cruelty, and every form of maliciousness. Out of apathy comes the willingness to let such things exist.

Now, when we confront the moral evil of mankind, we can explain it in just one of three ways: either it is illusory; or the Ground of existence, the All which alone is both good and evil (or beyond good and evil which, from the perspective of existence, means the same thing); or there is a real, even if not ontological, separation of this Ground and the particular beings who manifest the viciousness. If experience makes one unable to deny the reality and seriousness of cruelty and other evils, then either we must think of Ultimate Reality itself as partly vicious, or we must see mankind as a creature "fallen" in some sense into disharmony with the Ultimate. This last is the Christian view, and in choosing it the Christian sees three conditions of human life which, although not evil in themselves, present the possibility of that "fall" into evil which we observe to occur. These conditions are our creatureliness, our individuality, and nature. In pursuing this thought for a moment I am indebted to an interesting and provocative book by Hugh Vernon White entitled *Truth and the Person in Christian Theology.*

Man is a creature; he is not God. As a creature, to achieve his destiny he must learn humility and the acceptance of his finitude. As an individual, furthermore, a man must have some self-respect and self-interest merely in order to survive (a baby begins life with very little to recommend it except self-interest and an alarming capacity to express it). The combination of individuality and creatureliness, however, makes it possible that men shall explode their legitimate self-interest into self-centeredness and try to exceed their creaturely prerogatives. As a part of nature, says White, man is "a hungering, desiring, passionate creature before he is a rational mind or a spiritual person." [43] It follows from all this that finite, natural particularity—the human condition—lends itself to an exaggeration of the inevitable and proper self-concern so that this becomes a self-assertiveness which guarantees alienation from others and from God.

But if man is destined to develop himself as a particular selfhood, how can he do so *without* falling into estranging self-centeredness?

Teilhard de Chardin offered the suggestion that human self-development and self-denial should succeed each other, in a kind of pattern or rhythm, each stopping short of its own *reductio ad absurdum* but, at the same time, going far enough to counterbalance the other. It seems to me, however, that an insight truer both to the psychological possibilities and to the New Testament was offered by Søren Kierkegaard in his discussion of the "Knight of Faith" in his book *Fear and Trembling*.

Three of the most common attitudes that men adopt to their selves and to the world are self-indulgence, ascetic self-denial, and the middle path of moderation in all things. The self-indulgent man makes a primary value of the comfort, security, and satisfaction of his developing sense of selfhood, and tries to nourish it by meeting the desires of every appetite, or at least of those which he regards as constructive. He may, of course, eat moderately and keep himself fit, but if so, it is because the appetites satisfied by fitness are more central to his sense of identity than those which cry for mere food. He is, that is to say, self-indulgent in those things which most please him.

Very often the indulgent man seems to wish to protect himself from the onslaught of age and weakness by building a fortress of property about him, and—paradoxically—he actually becomes weaker through this maneuver because he identifies himself with more and more perishable things whose eventual loss threatens and diminishes him. If he is sensitive at all, furthermore, he may at last suffer the agonizing awareness that he has lived a pointless and trivial life.

By contrast, the ascetic tries to become free of all the claims that the world makes upon him. Where everything is transient, it may be that peace is to be found in renouncing everything. Long ago Epictetus warned us to care deeply about nothing that we do not absolutely control, for if we care about that which we may lose or which may be damaged or threatened, we make ourselves assailable.

> If you love an earthen vessel, say it is an earthen vessel
> which you love; when it has been broken, you will not
> be disturbed. If you are kissing your child or wife,

say that it is a human being whom you are kissing;
if the wife or child dies, you will not be disturbed.[44]

The man of moderation, on the other hand, tries to enjoy
whatever is enjoyable, but not to encourage in himself a dependence that would cripple or imprison him.

A defense can be made for each of these styles of life and
each of these ways of developing one's selfhood. But the
Christian way, as understood by Kierkegaard, is none of them.
The Christian recognizes one absolute claim upon his allegiance, and in response to the love of God for him he con-
centrates his own devotion in what Kierkegaard called the first
movement of faith: the complete renunciation of everything
else in order to be totally committed to God. But because the
God to whom he commits himself is the creator of all, the God
whose very character is love, the Christian simultaneously
makes the second movement of faith, which is to receive back
again the gift of all that surrounds and delights him. Consequently, he is no ascetic; he is no world-abusing, pallid denier
of life. He eats his steak with gusto and glows with the joy of
sun and wind. He dances life, and if, in doing so, he can command no more grace than a dysenteric duck, even this only
gives him something more to laugh about. He is sad, too, when
sadness is the season, for he is fully human. But in his weeping
or laughing, in his enjoyment of the world or his sorrow, there
is a difference, since the movements of faith were made. Because he renounced everything for God, he set himself free
from everything as the ascetic tries to do, and now that he has
received everything back from God he is free to possess without
being possessed by anything. Whatever he loses does not diminish him, for he had already given it up. Even his selfhood he
now develops in all its constructive potentiality because it is
God's gift.

Bernard of Clairvaux wrote about the degrees of love through
which a man passes to achieve the fullness of a proper Christian character. He argued that men first begin to love God
for their own sakes, that is, for what God has or can give to

them. In the second and third degrees of love a man learns to love his neighbors because God loves them, and to love God for God's own sake—not for the sake of what can be acquired from him. But finally the Christian finds himself loving even his own self (that is, seeking its good) for God's sake, because the full enrichment and growth of the self is God's desire.[45] Whatever one actually passes through to attain the ideal of Christian love, it is certain that Kierkegaard would have applauded the last phase of such love as Bernard depicts it. The Knight of Faith loves himself and loves his neighbor, not sentimentally (for he may, at any given moment, find neither himself nor his neighbor very attractive) but in that he seeks to promote the health and growth of mind, body, and spirit in each, for each is a creature who is part of the divine intention, his development part of the given destiny of existence.

So Christianity teaches neither self-mortification nor self-assertion, both of which are seen to focus undue attention on the self; it teaches, rather, self-transcendence through an ultimate personal loyalty to God, after which the development of the self falls into its proper perspective as a joyful obligation for God's sake.

Alienation, then, which is the root problem of mankind, consists in a turning away from the appropriate subject of man's highest allegiance and, as a consequence, a falsification of our relation to other persons, to nature, and to our selfhood's authentic development. Manipulation, destruction, and disarray within and around us are the consequence, and the cure is the turning back to the Source of genuine value, God, in a manner that restores to proper and healing perspective all our impingements upon the world.

The estrangement of man from his Creator, his neighbors, and his destiny is the situation to which the Christ came as a Word of invitation, compassion, and judgment. But that Word was never seen as merely addressed to the condition of first-century Palestine or to a preindustrial environment. It was seen from the beginning as an astonishing declaration about the future—the *ultimate* future of mankind. It has been said, indeed, that Christianity "is not interested in an event that took place at the beginning of time or in explaining why the world exists and why it is as it is. It is oriented, on the contrary, to a new future and hence wants to change the world rather than explain it." [46] If this is an overstatement in what it denies, it is nevertheless quite true in what it affirms. The Bible is a book preoccupied with the new, which is rarely if ever seen as a simple development of something already existing. Christianity was to be "new wine" which would burst the old wine-skins of conventional religion and society. There are references to the coming of a new song, a new name, a new spirit, a new covenant between God and man, a new and "living" way, and —above all—a new creation.

The work and the resurrection of Christ mean that the purposes of God will eventually be fulfilled despite the travesty of order, justice, and perfection which the world has now become. When hope is impossible because decay is universal, the Christian continues to hope—not that somehow everything will turn out well because the mess surrounding him was not real after all, or because he matters so much that an indulgent deity could not bear to see him suffer. No, the Christian hopes not for his own justification, but for God's victory.

There is a story in the thirty-seventh chapter of Ezekiel about a vision which that prophet saw one day. He seemed to be standing in a valley that was full of dry bones, as though an ancient slaughter had occurred there to men long forgotten. But at a word from God a wind blew through the bones and as the incredulous prophet watched they joined together again and were covered with flesh, to stand at last, living men. Then the voice of God explained the vision:

> Then he said to me, "Son of man, these bones are the whole house of Israel. Behold, they say, 'Our bones are dried up, and our hope is lost; we are clean cut off.' Therefore prophesy, and say to them, Thus says the Lord God: Behold I will open your graves, and raise you from your graves, O my people; and I will bring you home into the land of Israel." (Ezek. 37:11–12.)

In this manner the Christian sees the creative power of God as capable of a new creation. He does not look, lamenting, to a golden age in the past, nor does he think the present is the best of all possible worlds, but he sees the action of God in, through, and despite the events of the present bringing at last to fruition the hopes for which the entire order of nature was called into being. *For the future is the future of God, and because there is only one God that future will be coherent and unifying.* So man, in the midst of chaos and decay, seeing the stubborn hostilities of men and nations and the bitter disarray that we have wrought in nature knows two things: the future is God's and will therefore mean life, not death; and he stands under the injunction of God to renounce the easy path of apathy and, without pride, to become the stuff out of which the future shall be made.

"Much is done for man by nature; man can do much for himself, but his ultimate deliverance is in the hand of God. Evolution is a work of nature in time; progress is a work of man in history; redemption is a work of God in eternity." [47] But God's work of redemption will gather up the fruits of evolution and human progress, since all that is of value is conserved by God, and will give meaning to the work which man and nature do.

God so far transcends our understanding that he forever eludes the pitiful nets of words we cast to catch him, so that we must constantly have recourse to symbol, myth, metaphor, and analogy, and the language we have been using in these pages is replete with these elements. Yet, remembering the inadequacy of everything we say, Christian teaching points to the creativity and otherness of God as the grounds on which we may understand the condition of man in his world and hope for the creation of a new world of renewed men. Simultaneously we know ourselves to be entrusted with the task of spending ourselves to be creative, healing beings engaged in setting right all that is amiss around us in the world, for it is thus that we become participants in the divine enterprise.

X

Persons, Society, and God

Can the liberties of a nation be thought secure when
we have removed their only firm basis, a conviction in
the minds of the people that these liberties are the
gift of God?

—Thomas Jefferson

The essential grounds for Christian answers to all the questions raised in the first part of this book have been given or
implied in what has now been written. However, we must go a
little farther and take at least the first step toward the development of more explicit responses to a few of the most pressing
issues before we can be satisfied, and to that end this chapter
will be devoted to the following topics: the problem of significance in our personal uniqueness and historical existence;
politics and social order; and finally, can modern men believe
in the God of the Judeo-Christian tradition?

The belief in the creatorship of God means, we have seen,
that Christians must be deeply concerned with existence and
not simply "otherworldly" but that existential despair is ban-
ished from their repertoire.

Religions of the more naturalistic type interpret the events
of life on analogies drawn from the rhythms of nature, and
since (at least so long as we stand at a distance and look only
at those broad general laws which are the province of science)

nature is seen to be repetitive, the cycles of the seasons producing life, decay, and death in apparently endless reiteration, life
as a whole is understood as repetitive and cyclical. History
cannot, on this basis, be seen as offering the possibility of anything really new or unique. Of course, if one looks at nature
through the prism of a naturalistic evolutionary hypothesis, it
is seen that the new can indeed arise, but when it does its
emergence is unpurposive and it survives only if, by chance, it
is adapted to the environment efficiently. In any event, naturalistic religious systems are characterized by a fundamental
purposelessness, and it becomes man's highest hope to escape
the cyclical meaninglessness which must sooner or later begin
to depress him.

Similarly, monistic or pantheistic religions can scarcely take
history seriously because its struggles and events are "swallowed up" in the One which, in some fundamental sense, is
alone fully real. Here again, then, the human response is to
escape into a "fulfillment" which negates or reduces the value
and meaning of particular existence.

The Judaic tradition, on the contrary, lent genuine seriousness to history by its proclamation that the cosmos was no
chance assemblage of atoms, but the product (by whatever
devious path) of a purposive will which continued to work
within the structure of human freedom. And Christianity, because of its understanding of the Christ, provided a new dimen-
sion which shifted attention partly from the "corporate personality" of an entire people, which dominates most of the Old
Testament, to the importance of the individual and each act he
performs. In Jesus the Christ, the divine is seen as acting in
the world; the Eternal has actually (incredibly!) entered time
through a life that had a beginning in a particular moment, and
the Infinite has concretized his presence in the finite through a
life that filled particular spaces in the world. Henceforth every
particular entity and each particular action or event is seen as
radically serious, for to see them otherwise is to deny the
seriousness of the Christ. Here, too, is the importance of the

realization by Christians that the Christ can come only in one finite entity, for this is the way in which it is demonstrated that God is the Lord of the unique and unrepeatable event which gives meaning to all other events and raises their very uniqueness to importance. Because there is only one Christ, each individual matters, not just the process called "Mankind." Men are now not to flee their own reality in the engulfing vision of the mystical One, but to discover the meaning of themselves in the adventure of historical service of the Creator.

This means that each man who awakens to the reality of the Christ finds himself possessed of a terrible freedom. It is freedom because he is given authentic existence and room to act, and it is terrible because he now knows that his actions are significant, that they make a difference in the world and therefore represent something he is really doing to himself and to other realities. Moltmann has pointed out that the atheist tends to think: "Either there is a God, in which case man cannot be free; or man is free, in which case there cannot or may not be a God." [48] This would be true for religions of the pantheistic type or for naturalistic systems of theism, because in the latter, man's actions are merely part of the inevitable cycle of events, and in the former there is a continuity between God and man of such a kind that whatever one grants to God must be withdrawn from one's concept of man. But even in the Old Testament, God is seen as not the only Mover in the universe. He beckons (through his prophets) and man may or may not follow; he leads the people out of their slavery in Egypt, but if their courage fails, he does not magically transport them to the promised land of freedom. Thus Dostoevsky's magnificent "Grand Inquisitor" chapter in *The Brothers Karamazov* is splendidly correct: institutions (including the church as an institution) tend to inhibit freedom because they correctly recognize that people actually prefer security, but the Christ demands that we be freely responding persons and offers us only the strange security of faith.

What we have been saying, then, means this: as a singular,

starkly individual person my integrity is respected by God himself. But he offers me the unenforced privilege of fulfilling
and healing fellowship with himself.

Men, however, do not and cannot live in a vacuum, and our
freedom to act and choose our actions is therefore finite,
bounded and limited by forces that impinge upon us. The New
Testament recognizes this and teaches, if we may paraphrase
Paul in more contemporary but not more accurate termi-
nology (Rom. 6:16), that we will always choose those actions
for which we receive the greatest psychological reinforcement,
and this reinforcement issues from the connection between
our action and that object to which we have given our ultimate
allegiance. Of course, this presupposes that we have (as the
gift of God) some freedom to make a choice of allegiance, but
when we have done so we are pleased, satisfied, or reinforced
by actions which serve that to which we belong. Our objects
of allegiance vary—the comfort of the self, security, the nation,
the delight of the stomach, or the satisfaction of natural appetites, and so on, but once we have focused our loyalty (and
we may do so without deliberation, merely following some line
of least resistance), the actions we choose and enjoy will tend
to be those which fulfill it. It is even suggested by some
theologians that so compelling is the satisfaction of service to
whatever we love that there is no hope of our becoming free
to love something which excludes it or displaces it (such as
God) unless, by a kind of miracle, he himself acts to diminish
within us the grasp of our mastering allegiance. But even if
this is true, the Christian would have to affirm that God's
respect for our authenticity means that we can be given no
more than the freedom to change allegiances, never that he
forces upon us a new loyalty to himself.[49]

We are, then, individually significant because created so by
God. Without such a basis for our concept of personal meaningfulness it must rest upon the insubstantial ground of "common consent" or upon our "feeling" of importance, or upon
some idea that existence or humanness somehow carries its own

guarantee of value, and as Jefferson saw, these will hardly support securely the liberties men have tried so desperately to establish in modern democratic communities.

The individual significance which we have discussed, rooted in the appearance among us of the Christ as an individual, is significance (as is Christ's) in history and in the world. It is also more than this, but the point to be established here is that authentic Christian living can never be escapist, but, taking history seriously, a man must see the world and events in time as the arena in which he is required to act meaningfully in response to the God who is now the focus of his loyalty. This means that, as the great Reformers of the sixteenth century saw, ethics follows inevitably from the Christian's experience of his new commitment to God. We are not "saved" *from* the world, but *in* the world and *for* the world, and, to quote Paul again, so decisive are human actions and relationships that we find ourselves as Christians under the necessity of becoming "everything in turn to men of every sort, so that in one way or another [we] may save some" (I Cor. 9:22).

But for the Christian, ethical behavior cannot be, as it is in some other systems, a way to the overcoming of our lostness, a discipline essential and preliminary to the fulfilling experience of awakening or salvation. It is a consequence, not a cause, of our new loyalty to him who is the Ground of our being and becoming.

It is important also to note that the Christian does not act in kindness or love toward others because they are actually "divine" or because they and he are, in the deepest reality, One. On the contrary, the Christian loves others realistically as other than himself and can only love them in the sense in which the Bible uses the word so long as he sees their otherness, respects it, and attempts, in as much sensitivity and knowledge as he can command, to respond to it. For the otherness of God, implied in the doctrine of his creation of the world *ex nihilo*, endows all our particularities with authenticity and does not allow us to be sucked into a womblike anonymity of nondiscrimination. We are not simply expressions of a divine "essence" and we are not ideas in the mind of God: we are created in the "image" of God, and that means we reflect, as it were, certain characteristics which are perfectly fulfilled in God alone, among them being the capacity for self-discrimination and, as a consequence, for relating in a way which treasures the identity of others and takes seriously and responsibly the shaping of a real history in our working with others in time and space. Persons are important and love is possible because there is a mysterious sense in which otherness between them and between God and themselves is possible and real. This otherness, of course, should not be understood in the sense of substance; it is not necessarily (and it can surely hardly be) a genuine ontological otherness, but it is real because really established in its own domain and form by God. So pantheism is never a Christian possibility, whereas panentheism—the idea that all genuine existences have their reality within the infinitude of God without thereby being reduced to unreality— is at the heart of most versions of sophisticated Christianity.

Our history, then, is significant in Christianity because it is built of real events by real persons acting in real, although limited, freedom. It is significant, furthermore, because these real personal events are the material out of which a divine intention is to be realized, and in the truest and fullest sense of the word the Christian, and he alone, is the "free" man who flings himself joyfully into the stream not to struggle against it but to give his entire consent to its direction. Like Karl Marx, the Christian sees a determined end of history, and like Marx, he understands that the final freedom consists in moving with all one's heart and soul and mind and strength toward that end instead of resisting it (but helping to build it anyway with the curious blocks of one's resistance). But unlike Marx, he does not see the motive power of this end as autonomously in the historical process itself, but finds it in a God whose omniscience and infinite power mean that he can permit the rebellion of men to find expression and still weave a consummation from their acts. The meaning of the words "free" and "determined" are related for the Christian in a complexity that finally trails off into the mystery of God's being; but they are not simply or naïvely understood, for "simple" freedom or determinism alike imply the meaninglessness of human history, the one issuing in a chaos of wills and the other in a dehumanized mechanical process more like the functioning of a computer than a man. History is full of meaning for us because we are persons whose acts are genuinely chosen by us and genuinely make a difference to the world, yet the chaos of conflicting tongues and wills spawned by our arrogant building of petty Babels is, although real, not the final word but shall be found at last to be, astonishingly, a splash of color that finds its place in the splendor of God's consummated artistry.

If individual existence, on the one hand, and, on the other, history in the widest sense are both meaningful for Christianity, the interaction of persons in politics and social organization must have a place in the system of Christian thought. All too briefly we must next think about them.

The world is splashed with color and variety like a seedsman's catalog. The result, however, among human beings is conflict rather than delight. Human societies resemble a garden of contending flowers because distinctions have become an excuse for prejudice. In part this is the result of metaphysical presuppositions which men have held, often enough without reflection, which have led to the placing of certain kinds of value on particular distinguishing marks. For example, ancient paganism and some forms of Oriental immanentism assumed that what was, for any reason, held to be most desirable among human characteristics exhibited a high degree of divinity and whatever was less desirable was, correspondingly, less divine. In paganism the result is that "superior" men come to be divinized until they are cultic heroes or actual demigods. In India the result was the creation of a caste system. At the other extreme, of course, we have modern egalitarianisms that have a tendency to abolish not only distinctions of quality but every other kind of difference as well, so that one is bidden to feel guilty for alluding to distinctions which nature itself seems to have established and a proud woman strives to be her own man! If difference is to enrich our human culture and not to divide it, we must have a metaphysics that does not allow distinctions to be automatically degrading but that also does not oblige us to pretend they do not exist.

It should not be necessary to say more than that just as Buddhism attacked the caste system in India partly on the grounds that it (Buddhism) had rejected that idea of God which supported caste, so Christianity repudiates any version of caste because the Christian understanding of God liquidates caste distinctions. As Paul says, "There is no such thing as Jew and Greek, slave and freeman, male and female; for you are all one person in Christ Jesus" (Gal. 3:28). He does not mean that the physical, cultural, or even economic differences do not exist, but that the unselective love of God which was expressed in Christ makes no distinctions.

The strongest root of prejudice in the West, I believe, is not so much a metaphysical presupposition as it is a widespread failure of men to value themselves for the correct reasons. There is a pernicious tendency in most of us to acquire a sense of personal, class, national, or racial adequacy by attributing relative inadequacy to others. It has been pointed out many times that the most virulent centers of racial prejudice in the United States are to be found among lower-middle-class white people who find little in the social and economic circumstances of their lives to satisfy their longing for self-esteem. Economically they live a marginal or near-marginal existence. Socially they are aware of being near the bottom of a pyramid. How shall they, then, feel glad to be what they are without some other group to despise? They can like themselves only by looking at someone else and being happy they are not he.

So white men have despised and exploited black; the "Aryan" of ancient India or modern Germany had subdued a "lesser" race (the Dravidian or the Jew); men have dominated women;

the affluent have manipulated the poor, and some poor have abused their peers in order to become affluent.

This valuing of oneself *against* others has even corrupted apparent efforts to alleviate some of the marks of disparity, and this can most readily be seen in the phenomenon known as "charity." If I am rich, I give some of my money to help the poor, but I do it in such a way that while the poor are kept from starving (which would not serve my purpose, since I need them as a foil for my self-satisfaction), the circumstances which maintain poverty are not destroyed. Indeed, if a poor man becomes conditioned to accepting my charity and ceases to improve his economic lot by his own effort, I have the additional pleasure of despising his sloth without the necessity of recognizing that I have contributed to it by demolishing his self-respect through my patronage.

In addition to bad metaphysics and disruptive modes of self-evaluation, there are some other factors that complicate the struggle for a just social order today in the West, and we shall take space to specify two of these.

Another criterion by which we value each other is the quantity and, occasionally, the quality of productive work. The pride in accomplishment is so ancient a human trait that most of us accept it without question or analysis, and its fusion, since the Reformation, with a Calvinist work ethic has given it a secure place in the Western ethos. But what does it mean to value oneself or one another by such a standard? If a man is valued only for his productivity, it is the product and not the man which is valuable. Men themselves become mere means to material ends and as such are inhibited in their search for self-realization. In such a criterion we have the seed of a despising of oneself and of others, or of compulsive effort or, above all, of an enslavement of men to the technological and social machinery of production. With such a value system in mind, we organize our societies *not* to facilitate the fulfillment of persons but to maintain production levels. The consequence is a depersonalizing of each other as we become to one another mere extensions of the equipment we operate. This is to reverse an idea of Marshall McLuhan's. It is to affirm that in the modern West it is not so much the case that technology is an extension of man as that man is reduced in his own self-estimate to the status of an extension of the machine. In circumstances such as these it is to *production* that justice must be done, and even the massive destruction of human life in war is justified if it protects the impersonal means of production, distribution, and exchange.

It is probably partly a result of the loss of personal value, implied in the production criterion discussed above and equally operative on either side of the Iron Curtain, that another impediment to truly humane and just orders of society arises. Society itself becomes a kind of machine that must be able to absorb without disruption all the energies developed by its parts.

There was a time when men felt that the greatest adversary they faced was nature, and their social organization as well as their technology were means of mastering it. In one respect they were correct; man *must* master nonhuman nature or be destroyed by it. Today, however, most men feel that this battle is over. We dominate nature and bend it to our will (except, of course, for occasional lamentable lapses in the event of hurricanes, earthquakes, and similar imponderables). Today it is not nature that we must resist and tame, but the social and political orders of existence which were once our weapons and our defenses, and nature has become for many the great deliverer and ally to which one may run for release! We feel "imprisoned" in a structure of social expectations. We know ourselves to be swept along toward some end we are not devising, by social forces whose momentum we are not able to arrest. We feel like men in straitjackets being hustled by the crowd along a corridor whose end we do not know, and we long to be "free." So there is a new cult of the "noble savage" among us as we fight to escape a social impetus that we cannot direct or retard. Although I think it is an overstatement, one can sympathize with Jürgen Moltmann when he writes: "In the movements of the Hippies, of 'transcendental meditation,' of LSD-deleria and the like, I am able to recognize nothing other than such escapism." [50]

In short, the human quest for a just, peaceful, and enriching society is thwarted by the oppressive sense of impotence in a closed social system.

One response to the situation we have described is, of course, revolution: the use of any means to obtain the breaking of existing social orders in the hope of replacing them with others that will do justice to those who are presently oppressed. The answer, however, which flows naturally from a Christian appraisal of the world is revolutionary only in an importantly qualified sense and calls most seriously in question all the clichés of revolutionary dogmatism, however couched in noble sentiment with which to win the hearts and close the minds of the susceptible among us.

What is required, if we are to devise humane structures of society, is above all else a new way for men to value themselves and each other; a way which is above mere productivity by being more intrinsic to the human being as such, which can begin to operate remedially in a closed society, and which does not require the degradation of *any* other. Without such a foundation all political "remedies" are bound to fail, since they will at best salve only the symptoms and not the disease itself.

Nor will sentimental cries of "brotherhood" suffice to found a good society, for men are men and do not necessarily rejoice in being brothers. Since Cain killed Abel the fiercest quarrels have been fraternal ones and the bitterest wars have been civil wars, and the basis for a sound new way of self-evaluation and mutuality among men, if historical experience offers any clues whatever, must be profounder than a simple humanism.

We are affirming, then, that humanism will prove too shallow a basis for the healing of our social and political ills. And revolution, as usually understood, is so fraught with inadequacy that despite its appeal to the activism and egotism of youth it too must be finally disillusioning. But perhaps it is necessary to say a little more about that.

There are certain characteristics of revolutionary movements that must give pause to anyone with human wholeness among his ideals. Among these is a tendency to reject the past too simply and too dogmatically. When this, as is usually the case, is associated with the typical revolutionary puritanism, the ingredients of grave injustices are all in the pot. By "puritanism" in this context I refer to the tendency toward a kind of rigid moralism by which one separates men, movements, and actions into the good and the bad without real sensitivity to qualifications and degrees. As Moltmann says, "Revolutionaries often resemble the old Puritans who took themselves with 'deep seriousness' and forgot how to laugh at themselves." [51]

When this seriousness and too facile judgmentalism is associated with a naïve rejection of the past, you get an absolutizing of the present and, more tragically, of a particular "order" in the present. This tends to produce a closedness even worse than many of us feel to exist already in our societies and, as in the case of Stalinism, a persecution of honest and constructive criticism which is perpetrated by means of some convenient and malleable label ("Revisionist!"). The revolutionary may mouth allegiance to the idea of "continuing revolution," but what he generally means is making his world more and more homogeneous. He does *not* mean a willingness to allow those who come closely behind him to press him off the center stage and undo by their criticism any of his achievements. In this way the revolutionary, when successful, tends to become a tyrant as restrictive at least as the authorities he himself displaced. Revolution then becomes a movement in which the prefix *re* has a great deal of significance; there has been a *re*turn to a kind of despotism like that which was initially rejected. But this phenomenon has been so well caricatured by George Orwell in *Animal Farm* that no more need be said about it here.

Revolutionaries in our time face an additional temptation, not perhaps unique to them but more powerful today than in many former ages. We have experienced a general tendency since World War II to alter the style of our life from goal to role orientation. The future has appeared so uncertain that few can feel confident about projected goals, especially long-range ones, and there is consequently a growing likelihood that a man will think of himself not as building a future which he is able to specify with some precision, but as fulfilling a role (one thinks of himself as a teacher rather than as building literacy, the emphasis falling on a role rather than an objective). Correspondingly, revolutionaries in former times were usually genuine Utopians with a goal which they believed achievable and to which they dedicated their energies. Today, it seems to me, many are simply role-oriented revolutionaries—or perhaps it would be better to say "revolutionists." For them, performing the function of political agitator is important and "goals" are merely part of the rhetoric. If this is true, we have a uniquely dangerous kind of person because a role can, in principle, never be fulfilled. There is no terminus for it and no final satisfaction in it; it is simply the way one chooses to live.

Now, in the social and political chaos of the present, what stance is appropriate for the Christian? It is clear from the New Testament that although the Kingdom of God, to the realization of which he is bidden to dedicate himself, is not "of" (that is, belonging to, owned by) this world, it is inevitably to be *in* it. Further, the constitution of that Kingdom is based on a singular concept of love (in Greek *agapē*) which, unlike other forms of love is not acquisitive, is not a response to a desirable object, but is a commitment to a giving of oneself through the fullest possible understanding of the genuine needs of others. It entails a respect for the otherness and integrity of one's fellows that will not manipulate them or seek to reduce them to mere opportunities for enjoyment. It is *active*, not only lamenting injustices but working to redress them. The New Testament parable of the good Samaritan is a story of a man who finds someone desperately wounded on the road and knows immediately that the latter has been the victim of bandits. To linger is risky, and, furthermore, the injured man is of a despised and hated race. Without affection, therefore, the Samaritan does what must be done to help the other, spending time, energy, and money on meeting the real needs he finds, and doing it without the prospect of reward or the satisfaction of having liked the person he helped. With such love, Jesus tells us, we are to "love our neighbor" and even our enemy!

The immediate implications of the command to love in this fashion are clear. Since the most pressing and evident needs that add to the sum of human misery today are manifested in economic, political, racial, and international tensions and hostilities, it is obvious that the Christian cannot leave politics alone. He must be engaged in the liberation of the oppressed and the destruction of the conditions that perpetuate hunger, inequity, and fear. But must he, then, be a revolutionary? The proper answer to this, I believe, lies in a suggestion made several years ago by Arthur Koestler, who contended that the world could be saved only by a new "mutant": it needed men who would combine the qualities of the revolutionary and the saint. Such men would doubtless look with passion at all injustice and would find the revolutionary's abundant energy to seek and use appropriate means for change. But he would have the saint's humility to know that he was not God and dare not play with the lives of men as if they were pieces on a chessboard. Such a man would know that the perpetrator of injustice and racism is also a victim in need of love (though the love must contain a stern and unrelenting corrective impulse) and that the poor and oppressed are not to be idolized but aided. And he would know, because he had tasted it himself, that the remedy for the healing of man's alienating sickness of soul is available in a divine acceptance which liberates us from the need to value ourselves only at the expense of others.

When a man is neurotically immobilized and unable to function socially it is often because he despises himself without knowing precisely why. The things he despises in his own character are, as Freudians would say, repressed from consciousness because although they effectively operate in his life, to contemplate them would be too painful. Such a man may visit a therapist. It seems to matter very little what school of psychotherapeutic theory the counselor belongs to, but it is enormously important that he establish the right kind of relationship with the patient or client. It must be a relationship in which the latter is enabled progressively to explore his own personality more daringly and thoroughly until at last he has himself, as it were, out in the open. If he can do this in the presence of a therapist who does not reject him but manages to communicate acceptance of the patient (although not necessarily approval of all his characteristics), there is a chance that healing may ensue.

This therapist-patient situation is analogous to the kind of relationship the Christian claims to have found with a God from whom nothing is concealed, but who confronts us with limitless love. Such love is not without judgment and it is by no means opposed to judgment so long as judgment is understood to mean realistic, perceptive understanding. Indeed, it contains judgment, for it is not blind but entails a recognition of what we truly are behind all the devices by which we conceal ourselves from ourselves and from others. Without this perception it would degenerate into mere infatuation, but because of it, we know that it is *we* in our reality who are loved, and to be loved without illusion is to find ourselves provoked to a self-recognition deeper than we had known before or could have known outside the context of realistic love. To see, in the luminous mirror of the holiness of God, a reflection of our own inadequacy might seem to be potentially shattering. But when it is truly the Judeo-Christian God and not merely our Superego who confronts us there is, instead, a liberation. We are loved. The self-acceptance that formerly eluded us now becomes possible because of God's undeceived acceptance. And the possibility of authentic reformation also is ours because we have recognized ourselves in the context of love.

Henceforth the Christian is progressively saved from the need to value himself only at the expense of others whom he must devalue. If he is valued by God, he is free to value all that God loves—which means all that God has created. Little by little the *agapē* kind of love commanded by Jesus begins to become possible, for he can now love out of plenitude rather than out of an emptiness which constantly demanded that he acquire, possess, manipulate, and control.

Here, then, in this divine love is the fountain to which the Christian will be trying to bring the thirsting world. Having tasted it himself, he finds it difficult to imagine anything else that could cool the restless passion of mankind.

The Christian, then, will work in politics and in every form of social planning; but he will know that no such means can effect the revolution he seeks, for the only finally adequate solution to the total human dilemma is the finding of that common Center to whom our loyalties must be fully paid and who can draw us into authentic community in which differences which persist among us become enrichments of the whole and not opportunities for debasement.

Meanwhile, Christians should be active in every movement that even partly heals the social wounds of man. They will, no doubt, be more relaxed than the secular revolutionary, for they will have a larger vision which enables them to see the relativity of what they do and to laugh at every pretension to grandeur—including their own.

The Christian can find no final resting place in any form of social organization or politicoeconomic system, but subjects them all to a continuing criticism. Of capitalism, for example, he asks how the profit motive can coexist with a dispassionate love of our neighbor—a seeking of *his* welfare that is as diligent as the seeking of our own. And as he contemplates the cluster of problems, which are growing more acute daily, connected with the highly sophisticated technology we have devised—

problems of the pollution of our resources and the exhaustion of materials, to name only two—he wonders whether a free-enterprise system can find the vision and the authority to curtail "profitable" activities, perhaps even to suspend whole industries, which the survival of our species may quite soon demand. Of various forms of socialism, he asks whether they succeed in truly valuing the individual as a person rather than as a producer, and whether they do not lose his value in the collective mass. We must also ask socialism whether it really understands the limitations of human altruism and the need for the healing experience of being valued by the Source of our existence. The Christian cannot accept the state, the economic elite, the government, or any other human authority as final, but must insist that *all* authority, to be legitimate, must seek the peace and health of all mankind without distinction. At times in the past, and sometime in the future, I think, this makes him intolerable to the powers that be.

But whatever relevance this brief glance (no more than a signpost!) at Christian answers to the dilemma of our social and political chaos may have is dependent upon one final question. Can modern Western men really believe in the God of the Christian tradition? Remember that he is no simple totality of all that is; he does not stand as the one Reality which reduces all else to illusion. What is not God may have its existence in utter dependence upon him and (to use a spatial metaphor) "within" him, but he is the Creator of a genuine otherness out of which the marvelous richness of "I and Thou" encounters occur and all the joyous splendor of mutuality among men. But can a God who is transcendent as well as immanent, beyond as well as within us, be taken seriously by us today?

I suspect that most of us can readily remember ideas which, when they were first introduced to us, seemed not so much wrong as literally unthinkable. There simply was no place for them in the context of our intellectual warehouse and they languished briefly at the edges of our mind. Then, one day, we discovered that a rearrangement of our ideas had taken place so that the formerly rejected one not only found its place but seemed almost axiomatic. For many of us today, the idea of God is indeed unthinkable, not because we have any adequate grounds for rejecting it but because we cling to presuppositions about life, the universe, and meaning that allow no place for God and which would themselves be seriously questioned if the notion of God were to be accepted.

To many people the acceptance of a theory of general evolution has meant the forsaking of a belief in God. To think of man as evolving from some preanthropoid animal, and to view the entire cosmos as a development and process of some sort is, for many, to abandon the idea of a creative God. But one of the striking things about the fertile thought of Teilhard de Chardin is that he accepts and blends into a magnificent unity both the idea of evolution and the idea of a divine Creator. Indeed, starting from the premise of the reality of God, the evolutionary process actually becomes far more meaningful than it could otherwise have been, and Teilhard finds himself with a "singing" universe, pregnant with ultimately joyful possibility which may, it is true, suffer a painful birth. The "hominizing event," the emergence of Homo sapiens, is not a fortuitous circumstance; it is the clue to a comprehensive meaning permeating the whole business, and Teilhard looks forward to a continuation of the process of evolution until there shall occur a consummation planned from the outset by the God who nurtures his creation much as a gardener cares for his flowers.

The point is that the credibility or incredibility of the idea of God depends entirely on the presuppositions we bring to it. Modern men often have closed their minds on a few basic assumptions that preclude the reality of God, and it should hardly be surprising, therefore, if they never find him to be a compelling presence. Our presuppositions, conscious and otherwise, so largely shape what we can believe and what we can experience mystically or empirically that they must be subjects of frequent reexamination if we are not to suffer a lamentable closure to the possibility of new understanding. If, for instance, one begins with the notion that what is possible is limited to what is common in our experience, then God (and much else) is placed outside consideration. But the data which we use to form our criteria of the possible or plausible is itself changed if we begin, instead, with the premise of God's creative activity.

God is, according to Christian thought, "hidden" in his creation because only a concealed but present God can make possible and nurture the kind of free response which it is his desire to evoke from human beings. Too evident a divine presence would spell coercion. But he is there to be found, to be known in the immediacy of spiritual encounter, if we seek him with all our heart, accepting as the signs along the road the great events by which he has left his mark among us—the events which formed a Semitic people to be his priests among men, and supremely the event of his coming among us as his Word-Act, the Christ.

In an impressive essay, Gabriel Fackre has shown how the theological assumptions implicit in the Christian Sacrament of Holy Communion should provide a foundation for our thought concerning the approach of man to God and of God to man. He says:

> As the Christian Eucharist—the Lord's Supper—is a turning to God in and through the actions and elements of time and space and history, so too Eucharistic theology believes that Deity is met not in some private flight of the alone to the Alone, but through the grubbiness and glory of the time-space world, through the struggle to make and keep life human. As the Eucharist affirms the copresence of the divine and human . . . so Eucharistic theology welcomes the emergence of man and sees in, with, and under this human struggle the favor and power of God himself. . . . As the Eucharist climaxes with the communion of the human I and the divine Thou, so too Eucharistic theology affirms the reality of a transcendental God who does

not have to be justified by his usefulness to us, by
Gospel song or reformer, but is simply to be adored
for who he is.[52]

Fackre concludes that as in the Sacrament of Communion
the Christian, ideally at least, turns to God not to manipulate
him but simply to adore him for his own sake alone, so the
Christian learns there to love men not manipulatively or ac-
quisitively, but for *their* sake alone. The encounter with the
Christian God (who is, of course, the only God there is) not
only liberates us from undue dependence upon the world but
sets us free to enjoy the world and to work joyfully for its improvement and fulfillment.

Now, at the end of our examination of some Christian ideas,
we may summarize what I suspect are the most important of
them, since so many other ideas are dependent on these.

In an important sense Christianity is not a religious phenomenon but an antireligious one. A "religious" tradition, if we
may take our cue from the general characteristics of phenomena
so named, contains many elements but includes a system of
ways (or simply a way) by which man reaches for and attains
a revelation of the numinous. This, the "sacred," may be con-
ceived of as divine (God or the gods) or as absolute (Reality-
itself), but religion is the means whereby the individual and
the group overcome their ignorance or estrangement. When it
is ignorance that is seen as the central human problem, there
is a tendency for religion to become a luxuriant vine producing
increasingly exotic flowers of speculation.

Against all this, Christianity comes with a Word at once so
simple and so devastating that to believe it and respond to it
is to find oneself henceforth irreligious. The Word is that all
man's efforts, all the convolutions of ingenious theory, all the
formulas of the "religious" person, all the asceticism, the piety,
the forcing of brain and body to accept a demanding discipline,
are beside the point. Simply irrelevant. The transcendent yet
immanent God is utterly and irrevocably unknowable. He is
beyond our verbal nets and our imagination, and even beyond

the wordless reaches of our mystical grasping. Our theological systems and the breathless mysteries of the followers of "Theosophy" are alike ridiculous, laughable. His nature is Mystery-itself; *but he has given himself to us in an act which claims us as it forgives us and reconciles us to himself.* What is needed is very simple: it is to see that the eternal has penetrated time at one vital point; that the infinite has disclosed its love within a concrete instance of finitude. Here is the one essential miracle; here is the utterly absurd event that speaks to and overcomes the absurdity of our troubled existence. Here is the heart of wonder. Here is the Word so simple that a child can rejoice in it, yet so profound that its exploration will require a lifetime of sophisticated thought. And here, for him who sees, understands, and responds, is the death of religion. Now it is wonder, love, and obedience that man brings to God, and he is saved not only from his sin or from absurdity but from the seduction of religion itself.

Part Four
INCONCLUSIVE
CONCLUSION

XI

Comparisons and Conflicts

What you cannot finish you must leave undone!
—*Rudyard Kipling*

We have glanced at two great bodies of tradition, Buddhism and Christianity, to see whether there is any hope that they can help men to live in the tumultuous present and furnish material for the inevitable human dream of a completeness yet to come. Not all the problems that men face have been considered here, and not all those raised have been dealt with from the perspectives of Buddhism and Christianity. Rather, the attempt has been to show how a man might move within these traditions and deal with the kind of problem that confronts us all today.

It will be clear, I imagine, that the author believes that both the traditions we have considered are rich and fertile in suggestion, able to give their adherents a piece of ground on which to stand and a key to open certain ways of understanding which can offer exciting if not entirely unambiguous visions of human life. Perhaps it would be best to leave the matter here without having trodden deliberately the treacherous pathway of comparison. Certainly a book such as the present one would reveal excessive arrogance if it sought to make final judgments about the relative value of each religion, for these should be each man's own. But the mere outline of some ideas

in rival structures of belief inevitably invites us to compare and
evaluate those structures and to wish for a continuing dialogue
between them. Let us conclude, then, by considering some of
the ground upon which such dialogue can fruitfully proceed,
while leaving the actual business of evaluation and decision as
open as may be.

We must acknowledge at the outset that no interreligious
dialogue is possible unless both sides are respected. If our
allegiance to one belief system is of the kind that makes us
defensive toward all others, we can indulge in criticism of
those beliefs which rival ours, or we can be patronizing, but
we cannot really permit a serious encounter to occur. Can such
a dialogue ensue between Buddhism and Christianity, or is
there something intrinsic to either which precludes mutual
responsiveness?

Let us admit that a person who has found meaning and
liberation in *any* faith will not be perfectly objective about
others. But our question is whether the Buddhist and Christian
traditions inherently exclude intercourse.

From Buddhism's side it can be said that since the human
problem is essentially one of ignorance, and since this is a
phenomenon that exists in varying degrees of intensity, it is
always worth examining any claims to truth. This is especially
the case when the Absolute Truth attested by Buddhism is
beyond perfect verbalization, for another religious or philosophical tradition, despite apparent conflict of ideas, may actually be trying with different terms to express the same ultimate perception which is enshrined in Buddhism itself. Rival
truth claims are, then, not necessarily hostile, and the Buddhist
should feel it possible to engage in interested discussion with
advocates of other ideologies. Further, it is always possible
that other religions may be able to suggest useful techniques
for the attainment or apprehension of Absolute Truth. Yet
the Buddhist knows that the propositions which attempt to approximate Truth must be submitted to the light of the ultimate
Buddhist experience, and if they cannot be seen to lead toward
this, they are in genuine and decisive conflict with Buddhism.

Christians find themselves in a rather different position. The human problem is not seen, by them, as simply one of ignorance, but as a kind of rebellion—as self-assertion instead of response to God. Ignorance may promote this, but the problem is not merely to *see* the Truth but to overcome all reluctance to submit to it as it is expressed by the term "God," and to accept the humbling fact that one needs forgiveness. Yet the Christian, like the Buddhist, finds in his tradition grounds for eager exploration of non-Christian beliefs. Insofar as Christianity is a system of ideas and actions (a "religious tradition") it knows that it can no more adequately verbalize the character of God than the Buddhist can describe *Śūnyatā*. Further, even the Christian's belief that the saving event of Christ is unique opens him to dialogue, for he sees his own religious "system" and every other as companions under the common judgment of that event. His own Scriptures speak of "other sheep" who are also God's, and the Christian cannot automatically conclude that his alone is the voice through which God may speak.

Each religion, then, is open to dialogue, but each presents a touchstone by which authority is to be tested—the experience which suggests the *Śūnyatā* concept for Buddhism, and for Christianity the experience of God as he expresses himself in Christ. Interestingly enough, this emphasis on a decisive experience or intuition of Truth means that ardent adherents of both recognize the significance of Kierkegaard's dictum about subjectivity being truth and know that there are important respects in which a man committed to another religious experience may yet understand mine far better than a purely objective observer can ever hope to do. To study and record the observable data of a religious tradition is utterly useless for the purpose of understanding what the religious man considers important about it. Thus the dialogue between Christians and Buddhists may well be more productive of sympathetic understanding (even with strongly affirmed disagreement) than that between either Christians or Buddhists with disinterested social scientists.

So dialogue may begin. Its process, at least at the beginning, will consist of examining comparable concepts and submitting the differences to the judgment of whatever one has experienced as Ultimate. We can go no farther here than to suggest some of the comparable ideas and the divergences that seem to exist among them.

Nirvāna AND THE KINGDOM OF GOD

The terms "Nirvāna" and "Kingdom of God" refer respectively to the goal of Buddhist and of Christian striving. In what ways are these ideas distinct from each other? As soon as we begin to penetrate beneath the surfaces of these concepts important areas of difference confront us. The very words "Nirvāna" and "Kingdom" are widely separated in meaning, the latter patently indicating an experience of community under a supreme Lord and the former the experience of a passionless overcoming of distinctions. A kingdom consists of a system of relationships in which one must presume that some sort of individuality persists, whereas Nirvāna points to an essence that not only permeates all but is All.

Both of these ideas stress a conviction about the conservation of value: what is truly of worth in the universe is not lost. But Buddhism appears to consider the overcoming of distinctions to be itself a value of a very high order, whereas Christianity leans toward the idea that distinctions, although existentially ambivalent, are essentially valuable. Nirvāna, then, presents us with a splendid vision of unity, whereas the Kingdom offers us a prospect of community. The latter has sometimes been presented in excessively naïve images, but the basic idea in both traditions is not in the least simpleminded (indeed, it is the complexity and subtlety of the ideas, one suspects, that has led to their debasement in popular versions of both religions). An objection is sometimes heard that the idea of the Kingdom must be rejected because the sheer number of persons who have lived and are eligible for participation in it makes it unthinkable. To argue like this is to try to organize God's Kingdom on the pattern of Los Angeles—which God forbid! The shape of the transcendent community or of the communing entities is by no means prescribed by Christianity, and it must be remembered that a variety of ideas held simultaneously in anyone's mind may be thought of as a sort of community too. This is not to argue for a mentalist Kingdom existing in the cosmic Mind of God, but merely to indicate that the concept of community is much broader than one frequently supposes.

Unity or community: here are significantly different ideas of the final nature of the reality to which we move. But to see this is already to glimpse other related distinctions between Buddhism and Christianity.

PERSONAL OR NONPERSONAL ULTIMACY

Because Buddhism begins its quest for Truth by systematic denial of the ego, its progress to an intuitive experience of an Ultimate Reality results in a perception of that Ultimacy as nonpersonal. To be sure, *Śūnyatā* may be spoken of as a Cosmic Self, but this is not meant to imply personality. In contrast Christianity begins its reflection on the basis of an Ultimacy that declares himself in a personal event, the Christ, and consequently it usually sees all finite personality as derived from and an image of perfect ultimate Personhood. This, of course, does not necessarily imply that God is limited in the ways in which human personhood always is, but it implies that he is distinctly personal or suprapersonal, a Truth which must *reveal* himself rather than one which may be discovered by disciplined effort.

The nonpersonal character of *Śūnyatā* must not be thought of as implying a kind of inertness or "thingness" about it, for *Śūnyatā* is the dynamic but eternal Real, beyond limitation; it is the sufficiency of whatever is. Personality arises as its expression. But it would usually be thought misleading to describe it in personal terms, for it is experienced as outside the realm of the personal.

One may well ask whether sophisticated Christians do not

qualify their conception of personality so much in applying it to their God that the distinction between him and *Śūnyatā* is, in this respect, less radical than might superficially appear. Nevertheless, it is significant that although no qualities can be properly or adequately applied from our mundane experience to either God or *Śūnyatā*, personhood is felt to be a reasonably appropriate symbol for the former and an inappropriate one for the latter.

THE QUALITY OF FINITE EXISTENCE

Paul Tillich suggests that both the Kingdom of God and *Nirvāna* may be considered to reflect a negative appraisal of existence: the Kingdom is opposed to the "kingdoms" or power structures of the world, in which injustice is not merely permitted but, frequently, enforced; *Nirvāna* confronts all that *seems* to be real and valuable in itself as that which really *is* and which, when seen, dispels the mirage of mere appearance.[53] Yet there is a serious difference in the Buddhist and Christian views of existence.

The Christian, believing in a creative God, sees existence (God's creation) as awry, self-distorting, out of joint, but essentially as good and therefore redeemable. The Buddhist is inclined to see existence as something in the nature of a "Fall" from perfect essence into illusion-ridden finitude. Thus Christians speak of the "renovation" of existence or of a "new creation," while Buddhists speak of the cessation of the cycle of birth and death.

These divergent views of existence lead to different appraisals of the historical process. Christianity accepts the reality and significance of events so radically that God can redeem human history only by appearing within it concretely as the Christ. This leads to a tendency (when Christianity is not domesticated by prevailing powers) to drive toward the constant reappraisal and improvement or rejection of historical institutions in a kind of continuing revolution. For the Buddhist, on the other hand, history is "swallowed" by *Śūnyatā*, and "not transformation of reality but salvation from reality is the basic attitude. This need not lead to radical asceticism, as in India; it can lead to an affirmation of the activities of daily life—as, for instance, in Zen Buddhism—but under the principle of ultimate detachement." [54]

The affirmation of a somehow "personal" Ultimate, then, results in an avowal of the essential value of existence and a dedication to transform, renew, and improve it. The nonpersonal concept of *Śūnyatā* may also lead to revolutionary action and to delight in existent realities, but always in the interest of final detachment from and transcendence of existence.

Perhaps the difference in Buddhist and Christian interpretations of existence is most clearly exemplified in their respective systems of "virtue." The supreme excellence of character for Christians is that form of love meant by the Greek word *agapē;* this is not a sentiment but a seeking of the fulfillment of the neighbor as one seeks one's own. It includes a respect for, a responsiveness to, and a practical concern for the other, and resists all intentions of mitigating his "otherness" or manipulating him. Against this the Buddhist offers the strangely matched qualities of a love (*karunā*) which wills and actively strives for the enlightenment of all others, and wisdom (*prajñā*) which knows that there are no "others" to be enlightened. *Prajñā*, in short, seems to abolish the serious otherness of created existence, whereas *karunā* teaches us how to live within it.

These, then, are some of the areas in which Buddhism and Christianity seem to offer alternative perceptions. There are others, of course, but to consider the consequences of these few will suffice to sharpen our vision of what these great and living traditions have to offer as guidance for the understanding and living of our time.

Christians and Buddhists have failed, often enough, to fulfill in even a niggardly fashion the ideals they avowed. But the failure of men is not necessarily the failure of Truths they claimed to represent. The potential of either Buddhism or Christianity as meaningful orientations to human life can be assessed only as we struggle with their theological and philosophical content, try to understand and to appropriate the ground for this content, and finally consider its applicability to the problems and opportunities of the day. It has been the intention of this book to initiate or facilitate that kind of consideration.

Peace!

Suggestions
for Further Reading

BUDDHISM

Conze, Edward *et al.* (eds.), *Buddhist Texts Through the Ages*. Harper Torchbook, Harper & Row, Publishers, Inc., 1964.

—————— (ed. and tr.), *Buddhist Wisdom Books*. George Allen & Unwin, Ltd., 1958.

Coomaraswamy, Ananda K., *Buddha and the Gospel of Buddhism*. Harper Torchbook, Harper & Row, Publishers, Inc., 1964.

Kapleau, Philip (ed.), *The Three Pillars of Zen*. Harper & Row, Publishers, Inc., 1966.

Morgan, Kenneth W. (ed.), *The Path of the Buddha*. The Ronald Press Co., 1956.

Murti, T. R. V., *The Central Philosophy of Buddhism*. George Allen & Unwin, Ltd., 1961.

Robinson, Richard H., *The Buddhist Religion*. Dickenson Publishing Company, Inc., 1970.

Suzuki, Beatrice L., *Mahayana Buddhism*. The Macmillan Company, 1959.

Suzuki, D. T., *Outlines of Mahayana Buddhism*. Schocken Books Inc., 1963.

Zurcher, Erik, *Buddhism*. St. Martin's Press, Inc., 1962.

CHRISTIANITY

Daniélou, Jean, *God and the Ways of Knowing*, tr. by Walter Roberts. Meridian Books, Inc., 1957.

Farmer, Herbert H., *God and Men*. Abingdon Press, 1948.

Gilkey, Langdon, *Maker of Heaven and Earth*. Doubleday & Company, Inc., 1959.

Howe, Reuel L., *Man's Need and God's Action*. The Seabury Press, 1955.

Hunter, Archibald M., *The Gospel According to St. Paul: A Revised Edition of "Interpreting Paul's Gospel."* The Westminster Press, 1967.

Moltmann, Jürgen, *The Theology of Hope*, tr. by James W. Leitch. Harper & Row, Publishers, Inc., 1967.

Teilhard de Chardin, Pierre, *The Divine Milieu*, tr. by Bernard Wall *et al.* Harper Torchbook, Harper & Row, Publishers, Inc., 1960.

White, Hugh V., *Truth and the Person in Christian Theology*. Oxford University Press, 1963.

Notes

1. As we shall see, the word "religion" needs qualification and is, in some of its senses, inappropriately applied to Christianity. Here it carries its broadest meaning, which may roughly be specified as a system of belief and behavior by which one relates to a Value that one holds to be ultimate in significance.

2. W. H. Auden, *About the House* (Random House, Inc., 1965), p. 79.

3. W. H. Auden, *Collected Shorter Poems, 1927–1957* (Random House, Inc., 1966), p. 146.

4. Fyodor Dostoevsky, *The Brothers Karamazov* (The Modern Library, Random House, Inc., 1950), pp. 289–290.

5. *Ibid.*, p. 290.

6. John Updike, *The Poorhouse Fair* (Fawcett Publications, Inc., 1959), pp. 79–80.

7. *Digha-Nikaya*, 32.

8. "The Diamond Sutra," *Buddhist Wisdom Books*, ed. and tr. by Edward Conze (London: George Allen & Unwin, Ltd., 1958), p. 68. All material quoted from this book is used by permission of the publisher.

9. Reiho Masunaga, *The Soto Approach to Zen* (Tokyo: Layman Buddhist Society Press, n.d.), p. 10.

10. Yoshinori Takeuchi, "Japanese Philosophy," *Encyclopædia Britannica* (The University of Chicago Press, 1966), Vol. 12, p. 959.

11. Surangama. Quoted in this form by Beatrice L. Suzuki, *Mahayana Buddhism* (The Macmillan Company, 1959), p. 124.

12. Unpublished translation of Dogen's poem by Hiroshi Sakamoto.

13. D. T. Suzuki, "Mahayana and Hinayana Buddhism," *The Eastern Buddhist*, Vol. VI, No. 1 (April, 1932), p. 8.

14. B. L. Suzuki, *Mahayana Buddhism*, p. 47.

15. Eliot Deutsch, *Advaita Vedanta* (Honolulu: East-West Center Press, 1969), p. 85.

16. Edward Conze, *Buddhist Meditation* (London: George Allen & Unwin, Ltd., 1959), p. 63. All material quoted from this book is used by permission of the publisher.

17. Conze (ed. and tr.), *Buddhist Wisdom Books*, p. 89.

18. Pang Chu-shih, T'ang Dynasty.

19. Dogen Kigen, "Sho-aku-maku-sa," *Shōbōgenzō* (unpublished translation by Hiroshi Sakamoto).

20. *Majjhima-Nikāya*, 63.

21. Conze (ed. and tr.), *Buddhist Wisdom Books*, p. 25 (italics added).

22. Heinrich Dumoulin, *A History of Zen Buddhism*, tr. by Paul Peachey (Pantheon Books, Inc., 1963), p. 25.

23. Koun Ejo, *Shobogenzo Zuimonki*, tr. by Genkai Shoyu (privately published in Japan, 1965), p. 23.

24. Dogen Kigen, "Sho-aku-maku-sa," *Shōbōgenzō*.

25. Ernst Benz, *Buddhism or Communism* (Doubleday & Company, Inc., 1965), pp. 75–76.

26. *Ibid.*, p. 227.

27. G. K. Chesterton, "The Honour of Israel Gow," *The Innocence of Father Brown* (London: Penguin Books, Ltd., 1964), p. 119.

28. William James, *The Varieties of Religious Experience* (Longmans, Green & Co., Inc., 1914), p. 422.

29. Jean Daniélou, *God and the Ways of Knowing*, tr. by Walter Roberts (Meridian Books, Inc., 1957), p. 61.

30. Gordon Kaufmann, "On the Meaning of 'God,'" in Martin E. Marty and Dean G. Peerman (eds.), *New Theology*, No. 4 (The Macmillan Company, 1967), pp. 69–99.

31. Cornelius R. Loew, *Myth, Sacred History, and Philosophy* (Harcourt, Brace & World, Inc., 1967), p. 84.

32. Langdon Gilkey, *Maker of Heaven and Earth* (Doubleday & Company, Inc., 1959), p. 95.

33. Mircea Eliade, *The Sacred and the Profane*, tr. by Willard R. Trask (Harcourt, Brace and Company, 1959).

34. Jürgen Moltmann, *The Theology of Hope*, tr. by James W. Leitch (Harper & Row, Publishers, Inc., 1967), p. 141.

35. Daniélou, *God and the Ways of Knowing*, p. 106.

36. *Ibid.*, p. 14.

37. Gilkey, *Maker of Heaven and Earth*, p. 260.

38. James Sellers, *Theological Ethics* (The Macmillan Company, 1968), p. 98. This excerpt is quoted with the permission of the author.

39. Viktor E. Frankl, *From Death Camp to Existentialism* (Beacon Press, Inc., 1959).

40. Gilkey, *Maker of Heaven and Earth*, p. 217.

41. Sam Keen, "Hope in a Posthuman Era," in Martin E. Marty and Dean G. Peerman (eds.), *New Theology*, No. 5 (The Macmillan Company, 1968), pp. 86–87.

42. Moltmann, *The Theology of Hope*, p. 22.

43. Hugh V. White, *Truth and the Person in Christian Theology* (Oxford University Press, 1963), p. 154.

44. Epictetus, "The Manual," Sec. 3, in *The Essential Works of Stoicism*, ed. by Moses Hadas (Bantam Books, Inc., 1961), p. 86.

45. Bernard of Clairvaux, *On Loving God*, ed. by Hugh Martin (London: SCM Press, Ltd., 1959).

46. Jürgen Moltmann, *Religion, Revolution, and the Future*, tr. by M. Douglas Meeks (Charles Scribner's Sons, 1969), p. 5.

47. White, *Truth and the Person in Christian Theology*, p. 167.

48. Moltmann, *Religion, Revolution, and the Future*, p. 67.

49. It should be noted that to translate this discussion of freedom into the terms which we used earlier on the same subject, we should understand the reinforcing object of loyalty as referring to what was formerly called an "object of devotion," or that to which our "dominant sentiment" was attached and which gave "centeredness" and coherence to our living.

50. Moltmann, *Religion, Revolution, and the Future*, p. 185.

51. *Ibid.*, p. 145.

52. Gabriel Fackre, "The Issue of Transcendence in the New Theology, the New Morality, and the New Forms," in Marty and Peerman (eds.), *New Theology*, No. 4, p. 193. Originally published in *Theology and Life*, Vol. 9, No. 1 (Spring, 1966), pp. 49 and 50,

190 NOTES

where it appeared as Dr. Fackre's inauguration address delivered at Lancaster Theological Seminary on Feb. 4, 1966. This excerpt is quoted by permission.

53. Paul Tillich, *Christianity and the Encounter of the World Religions* (Columbia University Press, 1963), p. 65.

54. *Ibid.*, p. 73.